CARIBBEAN COOKING

John DeMers

HPBOOKS

This book is a fully revised and updated edition
of *Caribbean Cooking,* originally published in 1989.

HPBooks
Published by The Berkley Publishing Group
200 Madison Avenue
New York, NY 10016

First printing of revised edition: June 1997

Published simultaneously in Canada.

The Putnam Berkley World Wide Web site address is
http://www.berkley.com

Library of Congress Cataloging-in-Publication Data

DeMers, John, 1952–
    Caribbean cooking / John DeMers. — HPBooks rev. ed.
      p. cm.
    Includes index.
    ISBN 1-55788-271-1
    1. Cookery, Caribbean.   I. Title.
TX716.A1D45   1997
641.59729—dc21   96-49349
                                                      CIP

Printed in the United States of America

10 9 8 7 6 5 4 3 2 1

CONTENTS

PREFACE

There are many reasons for the fascination with the Caribbean that began with my first island visit nearly twenty years ago. The list starts with the same magnets that draw more and more visitors each year—endless sunshine, cooling trade winds, white sand and shimmering blue sea. Add to these a rhythm of speech and especially of song that gives the Caribbean people a lyrical movement found nowhere else on earth, and it's easy to understand the attraction this region has had over the centuries for conquerors, settlers, missionaries and buccaneers. It's also easy to understand why I love it.

From an early age, without realizing it, I was perfecting the outlook that would make me at home in the Caribbean. My father characterized my approach as "Always put off till tomorrow what you can do today." Nowhere has this philosophy been honed to such a fine edge as in the Caribbean. If Latin America is the land of *mañana,* the islands are the land of "Soon come." You'll hear these words again and again as you wait for an appointment, and you can believe them only at your peril. It's far better to grin, bear it and sip another piña colada.

Nowhere is the Caribbean more accessible than in the region's often spicy foods. They are the force that drew me there first and that continue to draw me back, whatever the emotional burdens or fiscal responsibilities of the moment. The very first hour of my very first visit sealed my fate, and it remains a memory striking for its clarity and intensity.

I had just arrived in Frederiksted on the island of St. Croix when the sunset ritual of the fishermen began. Women with woven baskets waited on the sand as the men pulled up their boats and started displaying their rainbow wares. Once the haggling on the beach was done, the men pitched their remaining fish into old wooden carts and pushed them up through the streets of the town, calling out each type in a lilting Creole patois. Women in brightly colored bandannas flung open their shutters and placed orders in voices even lovelier than the fishermen's call.

I was transfixed—there's no other word for it—by the pungent cooking smells from each window, by the island opera that filled the air, by the fading golden light. I had no choice but to follow a fisherman till his last fish was sold at the end of a winding path overgrown with bougainvillea and a dizzying look down across red roofs to the sea. I've followed many a Caribbean fisherman since then, on many a Caribbean island—and I've swapped recipes with many a bandannaed Caribbean cook.

Though no cookbook can catch that light exactly, or capture the shimmer of flame trees in winter, or evoke the icy tingle of a waterfall splashing into the sea, it can share the essential elements that make Caribbean cuisine a reflection of the people who prepare it so passionately. That is my goal, and perhaps it is tribute enough.

An Introduction to Caribbean Food

I invite you to consider Caribbean food a single, "national" cuisine, one with myriad regional and ethnic variations but increasingly celebrated for the characteristics that mark its special place on the map. This is not the traditional view, which linked each island for all time to the flavors set down by its colonial overlord. Yet it is the view that more and more reflects the sense of shared identity, the exchange of people and ideas, and the expanding appreciation of Caribbean food in restaurants from New York to San Francisco.

The Caribbean, in my view, is a single menu—even though its variations based on curry might seem far removed from its variations based on hollandaise. Not every dish on the Caribbean menu works equally well with every other dish; yet within the guidelines of prudent selection, there is a theme, a feeling, a sense of place that transports each diner to his own unique corner of the islands. Caribbean flavors can be that striking. Once tasted in their truest form, they will always be there for stability and reassurance, like a road waiting to lead you home.

Caribbean food is a marriage of bitter and sweet—not only in the flavors themselves but in the pain and progress that produced the union. It is an oversized cauldron into which generation after generation could pour frustrations and inspirations. As a result, the foods served from this cauldron bear the unmistakable stamp of many, many hands.

Arawak Indians were the first to call the islands home, crossing over from lowlands in South America. They lived, by all accounts, with a tolerance that put later colonials to shame, building small villages along the coasts and keeping to themselves. The Arawaks, no doubt, brought from South America many ideas on how to eat and at least one idea on how to cook—the beginnings of our barbecue. Yet for the most part, they adapted their diet to the products they found at hand.

They ate whatever fish they could catch, along with an occasional iguana, and relied for the rest on the produce that welcomed them to their new home—corn, sweet potatoes, beans, callaloo, guavas, pineapples and papayas. They also learned, from the earliest, that any hot pepper they could pick gave their meals an excitement they had never known in South America.

Indian lifestyles being quite different from those of islanders today, it is hardly surprising that few of these ancient dishes survive. Yet some are still among us. Home cooks still make Bammy, pounding the cassava, whipping it into a batter and frying it into a delicious bread. They still make Pepperpot, filling the soup pot with whatever meat or vegetables the garden or market provides. And best of all, they still spit-roast their meat and fish. Barbecued Jerk Pork has become a spicy Jamaican treasure.

Columbus "discovered" the islands throughout the 1490s, claiming most of them for the King of Spain. Yet it took more than a century for the Spanish to get serious about colonization. When they did, they introduced pigs, cattle, goats and horses, turning any wide-open space into grazing land and becoming important suppliers of smoked and salted meats to ships heading for the Americas. Lard melted down from animal fat proved the basis for commerce within the Greater Antilles—Jamaica, Cuba, Puerto Rico and Hispaniola (an island shared by Haiti and the Dominican Republic).

The Spanish, of course, were already proud of their cuisine and offered a cooking style as rich in flavor as their government was rich in corruption. As they did in other parts of the New World, these colonists learned as much as they could from the locals, mastering the Indian trick of smoking meats for preservation. But they also introduced a jungle-full of trees and tropical plants, including banana, plantain, sugar cane, lemon, lime, Seville and Valencia oranges, coconut, tamarind, ginger, date palm, pomegranate, grape and fig. In addition to these wonders from the Old World, they imported the best of the New—guinep and naseberry among them.

With all this ambitious planting, the Spanish changed the look of the Caribbean dramatically. And they changed its eating habits as well. Though they embraced barbecue with gusto, they also introduced frying to the islands, substituting animal fat for the olive oil they knew and loved back home. Escovitched Fish, one of the Caribbean's best-loved dishes, blends their technique for frying fish with the equally Spanish method of pickling (used to produce ceviche just across the water in Mexico). The colonists also came to specialize in dishes using beans and peas: things like stew peas, oxtail and beans, cowfoot and beans.

Through most of the Caribbean's early history, the languages and flavors of the region reflected the ebb and flow of Old World fortunes. As the Spanish came to dominate the Greater Antilles, other powers staked their claims in this strategic shipping zone.

The French, looking for places to grow sugar and coffee, assumed control of Martinique, Guadeloupe, Haiti and several other islands. Even today, the French West Indies dine differently from the rest of the Caribbean, mixing la cuisine classique with dramatic dashes of Creole. Many islanders still stretch the beef in beef soup with vegetables known as "leggins." Tracing this to the French *legumes* takes little erudition. And the memorable Patty, stuffed with spicy meat (and tinged with curry a bit later in history), also seems to have spread out from French Haiti.

Both Dutch and Danish scurried about for balance, the Dutch putting down roots on Aruba, Curaçao and Bonaire. A taste of the Netherlands is still available in the thick pea soup known as *erwten,* the memorable Edam cheeses stuffed with chicken or beef (Keshi Yena) and especially the pungent *rijstaffel,* a food fest of forty or more dishes transported to the islands from Dutch Indonesia. Denmark brought order to three of Columbus' favorite ports, holding on for 250 years until the United States bought St. Thomas, St. Croix and St. John. The Danish West Indies became the U.S. Virgin Islands in 1917, yet they retained their enthusiasm for what they called the "Danish table"—a buffet laden with wonders known elsewhere as smorgasbord.

Portuguese Jews arrived with the Spanish in the very beginning, and they expanded their population under each successive rule. These adaptable colonists specialized in confections; they turned them out in such volume they could hire native ladies to sing out their wares in the streets. Caramel cakes were among the most popular, made with imported sesame seeds. They also were responsible for introducing the eggplant, which became known on some islands as the garden-egg.

Of course, the Caribbean would not be quite what it is were it not for the English—300 years of them, in fact. In their own erring but well-intentioned way, they contributed much to societies that later became independent nations. And despite their often dubious cooking at home, they introduced a rainbow of new colors to every islander's culinary palate. Breadfruit and otaheite apples came from the English (breadfruit, in fact, from the *Bounty*'s infamous Captain Bligh), along with mango, rose apple, mandarin orange, turmeric, black pepper and the Blue Mountains' legendary coffee.

As it turns out, the English contributed far more raw ingredients to Caribbean cuisine than they did actual dishes. Rum is of British origin, giving the entire region a rousing pirate tradition and the basis for a measureless collection of colorful drinks. Roast beef is also ever-popular, though it often packs such a spicy punch it would hardly be recognized in London. The English did give the Caribbean a dastardly sweet tooth, guaranteeing that any collection of island recipes must tip toward dessert to be authentic. Cakes and tarts are served year-round, while Christmas puddings and Easter buns are relished in even the least English of households.

Looking back, it is impossible to overstate the rich heritage Africans contributed to the islands as we know them, albeit often under horrendous conditions. Slaves were a part of the Caribbean since the earliest days of the Spaniards, who true to form had wiped out the Arawaks within fifty years. Needing strong backs to harvest the bounty they had planted, landowners began the importation of West Africans from a number of different tribes—Ashanti and Fanti at the start, Yoruba and Ibo later on.

For reasons economic as well as racist, the Europeans labored to prevent their Africans from developing a taste for fresh meat. To that end, they forbade their slaves to raise cattle, treating them instead to salted meat and fish. Dishes made with these ingredients became incredibly popular, explaining the wide variety of uses for "saltfish" (salted cod) up to the present day. To survive beyond these handouts, the slaves planted gardens around their huts, doing especially well with okra and yams from their homeland, callaloo, corn, pumpkin, ackee and coffee. They did so well, in fact, they were selling their surplus by 1790 and using the money to buy salted meat and fish.

The African heritage is everywhere in the Caribbean, from the infectious rhythms that power Jamaican reggae to the graceful carvings now reduced to souvenirs. Yet nowhere is this heritage more magnificent than in the foods all islanders claim as their own. *Dokono* and *fufu* are two African dishes still found in their original form, the dipping of dough into soup or sauce being part of the collective memory. Rural kitchens are still outfitted in the old African way, with an earthenware pot called a *yabba,* a gourd called a *calabash* and a basket for smoking foods called a *kreng kreng.* Huge wooden mortars, used by the slaves to pound corn, are still found at the end of winding country roads.

Decades before the United States declared slavery an atrocity and plunged into the Civil War, the English quietly started legislating emancipation. Though the plan was based on hiring blacks who knew how to handle each job, the English soon found that most free men wanted no more to do with plantations. So a frenzied effort got under way to attract cheap labor from abroad. Small numbers of Germans and Irish accepted the challenge, but a whole social system seemed in jeopardy until the call was taken up by ethnic groups from Asia and the Middle East.

Indian laborers proved the most important group numerically—and culinarily—followed perhaps by the Chinese. The Indians found an enthusiastic audience for their contributions to the great Caribbean pot, since some of the English had already acquired a craving for curry in India. As the Indians rose from the ranks of laborers, they took with them the technique for blending pungent curry powders and using them to showcase local meat and fish. Traditional lamb proved hard to find, so a Caribbean substitute was drafted. Yet another memorable dish, Curry Goat, was born.

The Chinese and, in smaller numbers, the Syrians and Lebanese, added complexity to the cuisine. They certainly added it to many bloodlines. In the Caribbean, people of Lebanese-Welsh extraction are not uncommon. Or Portuguese–West African, with a bit of Irish on their father's side. To this day, islanders of such irresistibly jumbled parentage love nothing better than dining at a Chinese or Syrian restaurant.

In recent years, the influence of the United States has taken hold in the Caribbean. Especially with the growth of tourism, hamburgers and pizza have become at least as easy to find as Jerk Pork and stuffed breadfruit— and much easier to find than real English roast beef.

Yet for all that is lost when business demands "foreign" food, it must be said that a whole new generation of visitor is encouraging recognition of the region's culinary uniqueness. More and more Americans, surprised and delighted by Caribbean food back home, are heading south for a taste of the real thing. And more and more islanders, in response, are taking pride in the foods they grew up eating and serving them daily to their excited (if slightly sunburned) guests.

Ingredients

The ingredients used in Caribbean food, like the dishes in which they are showcased, quite often bear the most colorful names imaginable. Sometimes these names are the product of the islands' linguistic flair, while other times they reflect their wonderfully tangled heritage. Most often, though, the names spotlight a vocabulary pushed to its limits by the sheer wealth of items needing attention. The Caribbean's tropical bounty, it seems, has been quite a challenge for those entrusted with concocting tags for each and every variety of fish, fowl, fruit or vegetable.

To some degree, a similar challenge confronts those shopping for the most exotic ingredients in the United States. Of course, many such shoppers would feel deprived if the search turned out as quick and easy as picking up a pound of onions. Yet it must be said, for the reassurance of a different type of cook and shopper, that the vast majority of ingredients used by islanders are everyday grocery items in most parts of the world. Meat, poultry, seafood, vegetables, fruits, herbs and spices—what sets the Caribbean apart is less what goes into its food than the way it tastes when it comes out.

As a practical matter, there are three different levels of availability for ingredients used in this book. The largest group takes in items that turn up regularly at any good supermarket. Indeed, with the popularity and proliferation of tropical fruits and vegetables in the United States, this group gets larger every day. Exports from the Caribbean add blazing color to produce counters from New York to California, while U.S.-grown varieties of these wonders get easier to find (and to afford) with each visit to the local supermarket.

For all this impressive distribution, and for all the substitutions that make a cook's life easier, there are a few ingredients here that resist the most zealous supermarket assaults. If you discover a particular item is rare in your grocery stores, seek out a specialty market that strikes you as promising. Such judgments can be considerably simplified by identifying the Caribbean ingredient's origins. For instance, something brought to an island by the Spanish is almost certainly available at any Latin market, with the same system applying nicely to ingredients of Indian or Chinese origin. Flavorings loved by the Syrians or Lebanese turn up all the time in Middle Eastern food shops.

In addition to finding the items you need, you will find in these excursions an intriguing reflection of Caribbean cuisine. You will see, touch and most of all smell in these tiny ethnic enclaves the inspirations from which the islands created their masterfully different style of cooking.

The third and final level of availability is the one least relied upon in this book, since it requires a degree of planning that few cooks can muster and even fewer can enjoy. All the same, the mail-order gourmet route can fill in the few remaining blanks in any ingredient list, if you're shopping one to six weeks ahead. Probably the best way to deal with mail order is to isolate those items you can't find elsewhere but expect to use more than once, then order them to have them on hand. Presuming they are the sort of things that keep a good while, having them in the pantry, refrigerator or freezer will grant the cook in love with Caribbean food a spontaneity, which is at the heart of the true island lifestyle.

HERBS & SPICES

Taking the first bite of almost any Caribbean dish, a diner will realize in a none too subtle fashion that here are cooks who adore hot peppers. From the soup called Pepperpot to the pork called Jerk, the presence of hot pepper will be evident. That tradition of liberal spicing, in fact, is what has pushed Caribbean food from the fascination of a few to the virtual addiction of many in the United States.

Yet it would be an injustice and an inaccuracy to dismiss the islands' cuisine as the same old meat and potatoes loaded down with heat. As far back as the Arawak Indians, mixing herbs and spices for flavor was a beloved part of the local scene. The Spaniards added to the complexity of this mix, while the Indians and Chinese raised the technique to a tropical art form. It is important to remember, then, that many of the flavorings used in Caribbean food are grown right at hand. Indeed, many of the herbs and spices used in European and American cuisines are grown in the islands for export to those areas.

So embrace the spicy inspirations handed down from islander to islander and revel in the pungent aromas your own Caribbean cooking is duty-bound to create.

HERBS Be on the lookout for Caribbean thyme—it's terrific. And the islanders make sure it's terrific because they love it so much. It is by far their favorite herb, bought fresh in tiny bundles or inserted into a bunch of scallions. Islanders can choose between two types grown in their region, preferring the fragrant small-leaf variety to the broad-leaf "French thyme." Sweet basil is also grown in the Caribbean, along with several forms of mint and fever grass. These, however, are used more often in medicinal teas than in dishes for the dinner table.

ALLSPICE As though to keep things from being too simple, islanders call their single most famous spice "pimento," even though all other cuisines acknowledge its reminders of nutmeg, cinnamon and clove by calling it allspice. A tiny bit of allspice is grown in southern Cuba, but all the rest hails from Jamaica, where the berries are stripped from their branches and set out to dry in the sun. The English have long loved allspice for use in their pickles and marinades, and the Spanish have loved it even longer. In the Caribbean, it is an important ingredient in many famous dishes, a list led off by Escovitched Fish and Jerk Pork.

ANNATTO Orange-red in color and popular in soups, stews and fish dishes, this spice is native to the West Indies and the Latin tropics. Islanders often store their annatto seeds in oil, which then takes on their wonderful color, and the Latins grind the spice as well. If you cannot find annatto, saffron or turmeric can be substituted.

BLACK & WHITE PEPPERS Coming from the East Indies in the late 1700s, both these spices have found many friends in the West. Black pepper is the dried unripe berries of the pepper tree, while white is the ripe berries once their skin has been removed. White pepper is usually bought ground and kept in the pantry, but black pepper should be bought and stored as whole peppercorns. They will retain their flavor and aroma much better this way.

CHILES Hot peppers are native to the Caribbean and tropical America, as are sweet or bell peppers. They are sold whole, dried and ground or processed into lively hot sauces like Jamaica Hell Fire. Islanders use hot peppers with abandon, and they have a special fondness for the aromatic and flavorful Scotch Bonnet. Seek out these for your dishes first, perhaps in a West Indian market, or substitute the hottest chile you can find. Based on your own tolerance, apply whatever reticence you find necessary for survival.

CINNAMON In any Caribbean country market, you'll find little tied-up bundles of sticks and leaves. These are cinnamon, introduced to the islands from Ceylon in the 1700s and now a mainstay of puddings, porridges and other sweets. Islanders also favor the taste in their drinks and liqueurs.

GINGER This is one of the world's most relied upon spices, especially in the Orient. It was introduced to the Caribbean from the Far East in 1527 (by the

Spaniards once again) and quickly took to cultivation in the islands. The islanders use it not only with chicken and fish but in puddings, cakes, candies and ginger beer.

MACE This spice is actually the netlike covering of nutmeg, pink in color when just picked but turning brown with the drying process. It is often used in conjunction with nutmeg and cinnamon to flavor porridges and drinks.

NUTMEG Though most nutmeg is sold pre-ground in the United States, Caribbean cooks recommend that you buy it whole whenever possible and grate it as the need arises. The inner kernel of a fruit, nutmeg is more flavorful when freshly grated. Try it in cakes, puddings and drinks.

TURMERIC A member of the ginger family, this spice is called "too-mer-ick" in the Caribbean no matter how many purists insist on spelling it otherwise. Though quite mild in flavor itself, turmeric is the chief ingredient in curry powder, pulling together the pungencies of the other spices. It is also great for coloring, just like a mild curry or a pinch of saffron.

SEAFOOD

Seafood in the islands covers the entire spectrum, from flaky, mild, white-fleshed fish to those that are firm, meaty and robust in flavor. Crabs and shrimp turn up often, as do those wonderful spiny lobsters with everything but claws.

Though some people view seafood as exotic (and seek through shopping to make it more so), and others see it as intimidating, it is really one of the simplest ingredients to choose. Shipping methods that verge on the miraculous make fresh fish available daily in nearly every corner of the United States. Indeed, it's often fresher a thousand miles inland than three or four hours' drive into the Caribbean highlands. So concentrate less on finding the exact fish an islander might have on hand than on choosing the freshest fish that suits the recipe. Freshness will always repay you for your efforts; exotic seafood often stops being exotic the moment you try to eat it.

What follows are descriptions of the Caribbean's favorite seafoods. They should help you deal with menus when you are visiting the islands and enjoy great success recreating your best-loved dishes back home.

BLUE MARLIN There's nothing anyone can do to marlin in the kitchen that can equal its fame as one of the world's most sought after game fish. Each October, most of the globe's big-time fishermen converge on the Jamaican town of Port Antonio (Errol Flynn's old stomping grounds) for its annual marlin tournament. After the final toasts are downed, most of the marlin that isn't sliced into steaks and grilled is carted off to the smokehouse. The smoked meat is salmon-like in quality and holds up well when thinly sliced. When preparing salads or other mixtures calling for smoked marlin in this book, almost any skillfully smoked fish can substitute.

JACK These saltwater fish come in many colors, and they are as delightful to eat as they are sporting to catch. Jacks tend to be large, sometimes weighing up to 150 pounds. Names to seek out at your fish market include yellowtail, greenback, burnfin, black and amber jack. Most of these are readily available from the waters around Florida.

SALTFISH This fish is not as hard to find as it might sound. And interestingly, many of today's Caribbean cooks are growing away from the use of salted cod, because it took hold in the islands before fresh fish could be kept that way for reasonable periods of time. All the same, several national dishes are made with saltfish—ackee and saltfish being the best known. Often called *bacalao,* salted cod is widely available in the United States, especially in Italian, Spanish or Portuguese markets.

SNAPPER This fish, probably the most popular in all the Caribbean, is also a great favorite in the United States. Thanks to fishermen in Florida, snapper is available in fish markets and even supermarkets in more and more parts of the country. It is especially wonderful grilled, whether sliced into thin fillets or cut into thick steaks.

IMPORTED FISH The Caribbean has imported several fish in volume over the centuries and incorporated them into important native dishes. Mackerel and shad, for instance, come to the island pickled—as they do to many parts of the United States. Mackerel is showcased in the popular Caribbean specialty Run Down. Herring is imported, taking a place of honor in the dish known as Solomon Gundy.

CONCH Though land snails are most revered as the *escargots* from Burgundy, "sea snails" or conch also find quite a following when pulled by divers from the sea. Sometimes called *scungilli* by Italians, they are beloved from the Florida Keys to the farthest reaches of the Caribbean. Conch meat must be pounded extensively to make it tender (a job made much easier by the food processor), but its flavor makes it worth the trouble whether served cold in Conch Salad or hot in Conch Soup or Conch Fritters.

CRAB Crab and crabmeat make up a delightful part of the Caribbean menu.

Crab are wonderful simply boiled with pepper and other spices, then dumped out whole on tables spread with newspaper. And of course, the white meat cries out for any number of fancier presentations, from stuffed Crab Backs to Indian-inspired Curried Crabmeat. In the United States, crab are sold live whole, cooked whole or packed in one-pound containers, with lump being the finest quality.

LOBSTER The lobsters from Maine and Long Island seem to get all the press, but in the islands people happily dine on the clawless spiny, or Caribbean, lobster. They share their appreciation for this shellfish, in fact, with the people of Florida and the Bahamas. It is also very popular as the *langouste* of France, the *aragosta* of Italy and the *langosta* of Spain. Though the texture sometimes fails to equal that of lobsters from farther north, the flavor is nothing short of marvelous.

SHRIMP You see islanders digging into huge piles of boiled shrimp in no-frills restaurants along the shoreline. Shrimp are also served curried on many occasions, in yet another tip of the hat to the islands' Indian immigrants. In the United States, shrimp are marketed fresh or frozen in many forms, ranging from whole with the heads on to cooked, peeled and deveined. For shopping purposes, it takes about two pounds of raw headless shrimp to get one pound of cooked, peeled and deveined shrimp.

MEATS & POULTRY

Like most other cuisines at the everyday level, Caribbean cuisine is terrific at making a lot from a little. While freshness is always a major concern, there are few dishes in the island repertoire that require the most expensive ingredients. The people who devised this cuisine did not have caviar and truffles to work with—especially in the 1700s and 1800s, when even the wealthiest planters had to take potluck from England and the rest of the world.

Nowhere is this genius born of austerity more evident than in the Caribbean handling of meats. Even after the Spanish introduced animal husbandry to the islands, there remained more mouths to feed than there was meat to feed them. To this day, most islanders prefer slow-cooked dishes like oxtail and stew peas, a legacy of the days before tourists started demanding top sirloin. The slow cooking makes cheap cuts of meat tender, and it imparts their rich flavor to all ingredients sharing the pot.

BEEF Today, beef turns up in two forms more than all others put together: as steaks for the tourists and as hamburgers for just about everyone. Traditionally, however, beef appeared most often ground and heavily spiced in Patties from Haiti or cubed and stewed with a rainbow of island vegetables. Peas and beans were nearly always cooked with meat, even with tripe or cowfoot when times were hard. As is often the case in other parts of the world, these economical dishes became such favorites they remained on the mind and the menu even when finances improved. Today's Caribbean cooks weave many of these traditions into a broader and more sophisticated spectrum of beef presentations.

GOAT Islanders certainly relish goat, which historically took the place of lamb in most diets. Even the word "mutton" often refers to what natives of the French West Indies call *le chabris*. Sadly, most of the dishes using this tender and flavorful meat have passed from popularity. Only Curry Goat, a contribution of the East Indians, remains a common sight. It is indeed a welcome sight for the fresh and authentic Caribbean experience it offers.

POULTRY In years past, most fowl in the Caribbean were bought from itinerant venders known as "higglters." There were no cooling facilities, so poultry was bought live and kept around the house until it was killed for Sunday dinner. In addition to the more common, commercial forms of chicken, islanders love the savory country fowl called "sensey" (from the African name *asense*) and the Spanish "peel neck." Turkey and duck also have large followings in the islands, being roasted for special occasions but finding their way most often into stews, fricassees and pies.

PORK Few ingredients enjoy as colorful a history in the Caribbean as the pig or its predecessor, the wild hog. From earliest Arawak days, natives hunted these animals and preserved the meat on wooden grills. French explorers, noting that renegade seamen had picked up this trick, called the grills *boucans* and the cutthroat grillers *boucaniers*—thus the English buccaneers. Later on, escaped slaves known as Maroons carried on this tradition in the mountains of Jamaica, perfecting a peppery paste that made their otherwise boring diet a great deal more interesting. Today's Jerk Pork owes its existence to both Arawaks and Maroons. Pork is also enjoyed in savory stews and cut into ribs for grilling or chops for baking, nearly always with a dash of the piquant.

VEGETABLES

With plenty of visitation by clashing cultures over the years and a climate blessed with an endless growing season, the Caribbean has long produced enough vegetables to meet its own needs. In fact, recent efforts have pushed beyond traditional ackee, breadfruit and yam to compete in export with more advanced growing areas like Mexico and Florida. Bell peppers and cucumbers are the big weapons in this winter vegetable assault, though cherry tomatoes and zucchini are doing quite nicely too.

Vegetables have always been an important part of the Caribbean diet. They were readily available to fill in around meat when economy required. And since economy required more often than not, they became traditional elements in nearly every island dish.

ACKEE Jamaica is just about the only country in the world that eats this—nearly always with saltfish—though a few other islands grow it as an ornamental tree. Ackee is a red pod that eventually opens and shows off its yellow edible portion, which some say reminds them of scrambled eggs when cooked. It was brought to the island during the slave trade, giving birth to the legend that slaves used it to poison their masters. It can indeed be deadly if eaten before fully mature, so wait for the pod to open in its own good time. Available fresh or frozen in the Caribbean, ackee is mostly exported in cans.

BANANA & PLANTAIN Though often thought of as fruits, bananas and their close relation plantains technically weigh in as vegetables. They are certainly eaten often enough to be both in the Caribbean, where their traditional uses at the end of a meal are bolstered by various appearances in nearly every other course. When used green, bananas can be simply boiled as a side dish or made into porridge, dumplings, puddings or Run Down (another island classic using saltfish). Once ripe, they can be combined with fruits to make salads, desserts and beverages. Unlike the banana, the plantain should not be eaten raw even when it is ripe. Green plantains are usually boiled in soups, while ripe ones are quite good fried.

BREADFRUIT Captain Bligh of *Bounty* fame was responsible for introducing breadfruit to the islands in 1793, spreading it from its home in Tahiti. It grew so well in the Caribbean that it found its way into an incredible array of uses. The blossoms (or swords) are great in preserves, and the mature fruit is served boiled, roasted after being stuffed with meat, or as a salad, pudding, flour, chips or even as a beverage. As though that were not enough, the leaves are used for feeding cattle and the wood for making furniture.

CALLALOO This colorful name turns up in literature as early as 1696, evolving since then through innumerable spellings and almost as many recipes. Yet it's always the same wonderful spinachlike vegetable, one of the chief ingredients in the famed Pepperpot Soup. This preparation, by the way, should not be confused with the Callaloo Soup of the eastern Caribbean, which is made from the leaves of the dasheen plant.

CHAYOTE This vegetable that grows on a luxuriant vine goes by many names across the tropical Americas—cho-cho, christophene, bironne, custard marrow, vegetable pear, pepinella and mirleton. A larger relative of the cucumber, chayote is either boiled to serve alongside meats or added to soups and stews. Islanders have long known that with the addition of a little lime juice, it is also a fine substitute for apples in pies and tarts.

CORN This vegetable was one of the first to grow in the Caribbean, feeding populations as early as the Arawaks. It is most often called maize or Indian corn, confirming its roots in tropical America, and is enjoyed grilled or boiled in peppery water. Cornmeal is also popular in the Caribbean, its uses ranging widely from dumplings to West African *dokono,* often called Tie-a-Leaf.

PEAS & BEANS Caribbean natives certainly adore these things, most often in the national dish called Rice & Peas. The red pea (or kidney bean) is probably the islands' most popular, with a small variety going into Rice & Peas and a large type turning up in soups and stews. Gungo (or pigeon) peas, introduced from West Africa by the Spaniards, are enjoyed regularly as well. Cow peas and black-eyed peas are often substituted for gungo, while butter, broad and lima beans are used in oxtail and beans, Cowfoot & Beans and Tripe & Beans.

TUBERS Members of this valuable family used in Caribbean cuisine include yams, sweet potatoes, so-called Irish potatoes, cassava and coco. Yams almost certainly made the crossing from Africa—they were filling food for slaves. Many Caribbean recipes still showcase them today, especially the varieties known as Lucea, St. Vincent and Barbados. The sweet potato originally came from India. It is most often baked or candied, used in salads, puddings or pies, or served as an accompaniment to meats. The Irish potato is the familiar white tuber, native to Ecuador but later taken to Spain and the British Isles. It is mainly used as a vegetable side dish, though it can turn up mashed in desserts or beverages. Cassava goes back to the time of the Arawaks, making possible such products as starch, tapioca, farina and cassava meal (not to mention Bammy, the incredible fried bread beloved throughout the islands). Coco, also known as taro and tannia, is a starchy tuber usually boiled or added to hearty soups.

Fruits

From the dirt farmer munching a mango outside his hut to the socialite feasting on Trifle in a luxury hotel, islanders adore fresh fruit to a degree equaled only by its abundance on their islands. The beaches, the valleys, even the mountainsides are crazy with this bounty—bursting open, ripening, taking on color in the warm, moist air.

Cooks in the United States are fortunate that most tropical fruits grow in such volume and travel with such ease that they are increasingly available nationwide. Oranges, pineapples, lemons and limes are grown domestically, of course. More and more, the same can be said of coconuts, mango and papayas. What few Caribbean fruits resist turning up in mainstream U.S. supermarkets often appear in Latin or West Indian food shops.

AVOCADO These were once known around the Caribbean as "midshipman's butter" or "poor man's butter." Today the islanders simply call them "pears," making for confusion with the fruit enjoyed in the United States. Avocados with either green or purple skins are grown in the islands as well as in Mexico and other parts of Latin America. California does a great job with them as well. They are a delightful ingredient in fruit and vegetable salads and can be made into a delicious tropical paste (as any lover of Mexican guacamole will readily avow).

COCONUT A member of the palm family that adds so much to the look and feel of the Caribbean, the coconut hails from Malaysia but has taken with gusto to the western tropics. It yields fruit all year round and is edible in both its green and mature stages. The so-called "water" and "jelly" in the green coconut are delightful, with the former finding its way into numerous island drinks. The mature fruit is used in many Caribbean dishes, especially in sweets.

GRAPEFRUIT There are many experts who believe the grapefruit originated in Jamaica. It is well-established on that island, and it was so when no other place growing citrus fruits had even heard of it. The name is said to reflect the perceived taste similarity between the grapefruit and the grape, rather than the sight of the fruit hanging in clusters.

GUAVA Indigenous to the Caribbean, guava has an enthusiastic following. It grows everywhere in the islands and lends itself quite well to jellies, preserves, fruit cups, wines, cocktails and desserts. It is also delicious when eaten raw.

LEMONS & LIMES The flavor of these two widely cultivated citrus fruits is enjoyed in beverages, cakes and preserves, as well as with chicken and fish.

The lime grew in importance when it was identified as both a preservative and as a cure for the scurvy afflicting the British Navy.

MANGO Called the "peach of the tropics," this fruit was actually discovered in the shadow of the Himalayas. It was successfully transplanted from there to such warmer climates as India, China, Latin America and the Caribbean. Mango is flavorful all by itself or used with other fruits in salads or desserts. The best varieties are the Bombay, East Indian, St. Julian and Hayden.

ORANGES There seem to be almost as many types of oranges as there are oranges, but they generally can be placed in one of two categories—bitter or sweet. The rather acidic Valencia and Seville made the crossing from Spain to find a place in sweetened beverages and marmalades. Island farmers developed quite a few other varieties, including ortanique, naval and one called ugly.

PAPAYA Islanders call this "pawpaw" and eat it by that or any other name as often as possible. A native of South America, the fruit is orange-colored when ripe and tends in flavor toward the bland. Yet it benefits richly from association with fruits having sharper flavors. It makes a good Caribbean drink sweetened with condensed milk or sugar, and the green fruit is sometimes served as a vegetable.

PINEAPPLE This fruit, called most often simply "pine" in the islands, is believed to have originated in Central America and the Caribbean. It is as versatile as foods come, finding many tastes and textures in a host of desserts along with meat and seafood specialties. It is also great eaten fresh, all by itself.

OTHER FRUITS There's a rainbow of other fruits adding color and flavor to Caribbean cuisine. Among the most significant are naseberry, star apple (or carambola), otaheite apple, passion fruit, West Indian garden cherry, jackfruit, soursop and tamarind.

BASICS

The recipes in this chapter are for those ingredients such as rich stocks that enhance the
flavors of Caribbean cooking. Because the flavors of coconut and curry are popular in many
dishes, recipes for making your own Curry
Powder and Coconut Milk are included.

HOLLANDAISE SAUCE

Here is a basic hollandaise recipe that works well not only browned atop La Barquilla de Piña but spooned over vegetable side dishes from asparagus to broccoli.

4 egg yolks
1 cup butter
1/4 cup hot water
1/4 cup lemon juice
1/4 teaspoon salt
1 pinch of red (cayenne) pepper

Beat the egg yolks thoroughly in a small bowl. Melt butter over low heat until it bubbles, but do not let it brown. Slowly pour melted butter into egg yolks while beating constantly. Add hot water, still stirring. Pour from bowl into a double boiler over warm water to keep warm. Stir in lemon juice, salt and cayenne. *Makes about 2 cups.*

MANGO CHUTNEY

Indian laborers would never have eaten their curries without chutneys. Today, every Caribbean cook seems to have his or her own chutney recipe.

8 large unripe mangoes
1 tablespoon salt
2 Scotch Bonnet or jalapeño chiles
3 cups malt vinegar
5 garlic cloves
1/2 cup peeled, chopped gingerroot
1 cup sugar
1-1/2 cups seedless raisins

Peel and slice mangoes, discarding seeds, then place slices in a large bowl and sprinkle with salt. Trim stalks from chiles; remove seeds. Soak peppers in a little of vinegar about 10 minutes, then process them in a blender with garlic and gingerroot until minced. Pour remaining vinegar into a saucepan; add blended mixture and sugar. Bring to a boil, then reduce heat and simmer, uncovered, 15 minutes. Add mangoes and raisins; simmer until thick and syrupy. Cool and spoon chutney into sterile jars. Seal with airtight lids. Process in a water bath 5 minutes. *Makes about 8 pints.*

TURKEY STOCK

Good turkey stock is richer in flavor than chicken stock, yet it can be "stretched" by adding chicken stock if you need more liquid for your soup.

1 turkey carcass
2 carrots, coarsely chopped
2 parsley sprigs
2 onions, quartered
3 celery tops
2 teaspoons salt
1 teaspoon freshly ground black pepper
1 bay leaf
1/4 teaspoon dried leaf thyme
2 garlic cloves

Break carcass into pieces; place in a large pot. Add all remaining ingredients and enough water to cover. Bring to a boil, then reduce heat, cover and simmer at least 4 hours but preferably overnight. Strain stock through a colander or cheesecloth. Refrigerate covered until fat congeals on top, then skim off fat. *Makes about 2 quarts.*

CHICKEN STOCK

Homemade stock is the hands-down winner over canned broth. If you have too few bones from preparing a single meal, just toss what you have into a plastic bag in the freezer until you have enough. The stock itself can be refrigerated for several days, or it can be frozen until you need it.

1 carcass from chicken
2 carrots, coarsely chopped
2 parsley sprigs
2 onions, quartered
3 celery tops
2 teaspoons salt
1 teaspoon freshly ground black pepper
1 bay leaf
1/4 teaspoon thyme
2 garlic cloves

Break chicken carcass into pieces. Add these to a large pot; add all remaining ingredients. Cover with water. Bring to a boil, then reduce heat, cover and simmer 4 hours or more. Overnight simmering will produce an even richer flavor. Strain stock through a colander or cheesecloth into a large bowl. Cover and refrigerate until fat hardens on top, then skim off fat. *Makes 2 quarts.*

BEEF STOCK

Here's a good basic recipe for beef stock. It can be refrigerated for several days or frozen for use as needed.

1 pound beef shanks, in pieces
3 pounds beef soup bones
2 medium carrots, quartered
2 medium onions, quartered
3 celery stalks, coarsely chopped
2 leeks, coarsely chopped
2 garlic cloves, crushed
5 parsley sprigs
2 bay leaves
1 tablespoon freshly ground black pepper
2 teaspoons salt
1 cup dry white wine
4 quarts cold water

Combine all ingredients in a large stockpot. Bring to a boil, skimming off froth as it rises to surface. Reduce heat and simmer partially covered at least 4 hours, making sure stock does not boil. Take out all bones and strain stock through a sieve, then skim off as much fat as you can. *Makes about 2 quarts.*

FISH STOCK

It's no big burden to make your own fish stock. Often you can make enough stock just from the bones of the fish you are cooking. Or you can make a lot and keep it handy in the freezer up to one month, perhaps cubed in ice trays so you can use only what you need.

2 pounds fish bones, rinsed
2 medium onions, quartered
1/2 leek, chopped
3 celery stalks, chopped
1/4 bunch parsley, chopped
1 pinch of dried leaf thyme
1 bay leaf
1 teaspoon freshly ground black pepper
1 cup white wine

Place fish bones and all vegetables and seasonings in a large stockpot. Add wine and enough water to cover and bring to a boil. Reduce heat and simmer 1 hour, until volume is reduced by about 1/2. Remove from heat, skim and cool. Strain before using. *Makes about 1 quart.*

COCONUT MILK

Yes, it is possible to buy coconut milk in cans. But not only is it a bit exotic to meet a real coconut "face to face"—the fresh milk is always more flavorful.

1 fresh coconut
Water

Crack coconut and drain liquid into a measuring cup. Remove meat and cut into 1/2-inch pieces. Add enough water to liquid in measuring cup to make 1/2 cup. Add coconut meat and liquid to a blender or food processor fitted with the steel blade. Process until pureed. Place puree in a saucepan and heat gently. Let steep 30 minutes, then strain through a double thickness of cheesecloth.   *One coconut makes about 1/2 cup of coconut milk.*

CURRY POWDER

A desire for absolute freshness and individuality inspires most faithful Indian cooks to blend their own curry powder. Here is a good basic recipe that will work in all the curry-laced recipes in this book.

4 teaspoons coriander seeds
4 teaspoons ground turmeric
1 teaspoon ground fenugreek
4 teaspoons ground ginger
4 teaspoons ground black pepper
1 teaspoon ground cardamom
1 teaspoon ground cinnamon

Mix all these ingredients together. Store in an airtight jar.   *Makes about 6 tablespoons.*

Appetizers

When it comes to Caribbean appetizers, it truly seems there's no accounting for taste. From island to island, even from cook to cook, an appetizer can mean just about anything, from the simplest little nibble set out in a bowl to a full-blown creation served as an opening course, such as Smoked Marlin Salad. In general, though, Caribbean appetizers tend to emphasize flavor and color over stuffy formality. From Patties, which require and repay a good bit of effort, to the breezy Hot Pepper Coconut, there's little attempt in these dishes to impress except through fresh ingredients and good ideas. Many of the islands' favorite appetizers, it turns out, are grown-up versions of "street food," things people became accustomed to munching as children and never forgot. This means your appetizer, however you choose to present it, can be both authentic and memorable.

STAMP & GO

According to the Jamaicans, Stamp & Go gets its colorful name because it's a favored snack at bus stops all over the island. Riders can hop off their bus, inhale this tasty treat and climb back to continue their trip. This action, in the Caribbean's lyrical lingo is described as "stamp and go."

1/4 pound salt codfish
6 tablespoons boiling water
1/2 cup all-purpose flour
1 onion, finely chopped
1 garlic clove, finely chopped
1 tablespoon seeded, chopped Scotch Bonnet or jalapeño chile
1 tablespoon finely chopped chives
Salt and freshly ground black pepper to taste
1/2 teaspoon finely chopped fresh thyme
2 eggs, separated
Vegetable oil for deep-frying
1 teaspoon tarragon-flavored vinegar

Soak salt codfish in water several hours, or preferably overnight. Drain; pour the boiling water over fish and cool. Drain off water and slowly combine it with flour in a bowl, stirring until mixture is smooth. Rinse fish in fresh cold water, remove any skin and bones, then shred very finely. Add fish, onion, garlic, chile, chives, salt, black pepper, thyme and egg yolks to flour mixture. Stir until combined.

Heat oil in a deep skillet to 375F (190C) or until a 1-inch bread cube turns golden brown in 50 seconds. Beat egg whites until stiff but not dry; fold into fish mixture along with vinegar. Drop this batter by tablespoons into hot oil; fry until golden brown. Drain on paper towels and serve hot. *Makes 6 servings.*

Rio Cobre Crepes

While the rolling of crepes around fillings remains more European than Caribbean, no island chef would fail to make this filling his own.

1 pound red kidney beans, soaked overnight
1 quart Beef Stock (page 24)
1/2 cup chopped onion
1/4 cup chopped green onion
1 teaspoon finely chopped fresh thyme
1 teaspoon finely chopped garlic
1/2 cup Coconut Milk (page 26)
6 bacon slices, crisp-cooked, crumbled
Salt and freshly ground black pepper to taste
2 tablespoons cornstarch dissolved in 2 tablespoons water

CREPES

1 cup milk
1/2 cup all-purpose flour
2 eggs
1/2 teaspoon baking powder
1/2 teaspoon salt
Butter or margarine

In a large saucepan, cook kidney beans in stock until soft, about 1-1/2 hours. Add onion, green onion, thyme, garlic, Coconut Milk and bacon, then simmer 10 minutes. Season to taste with salt and freshly ground black pepper. Thicken with cornstarch mixture. Meanwhile, prepare Crepes. Place a portion of bean mixture on each crepe and roll crepe around it. Set 2 crepes on each of 6 appetizer plates. Serve hot. *Makes 6 servings.*

CREPES

To prepare crepes, stir milk and flour together in a medium bowl. Beat in eggs, baking powder and salt, beating until smooth. Melt 1 tablespoon butter in a 6-inch crepe pan. Pour a thin layer of batter into pan. Cook until browned on bottom; turn and cook other side until lightly browned. Repeat with remaining batter, adding more butter as needed. *Makes 12 crepes.*

Black-Eyed Pea Salad

Peas and beans have played a large role in every Caribbean diet since the very earliest times. Here's a recipe that should push aside any other bean salad you've tried.

1 cup black-eyed peas
1 tablespoon vegetable oil
1 medium onion, chopped
1 garlic clove, chopped
2 tablespoons tomato paste
1/4 pound boiled shrimp, peeled, deveined, chopped
1/4 pound ham, diced
Salt to taste
1 tablespoon lemon juice

Combine peas and enough water to cover by 2 inches in a medium saucepan. Bring to a boil, reduce heat and simmer 45 minutes, then drain them well. Heat oil in a medium skillet over medium heat. Add onion and garlic; cook until soft but not browned. Stir in tomato paste, shrimp and ham. When these are just heated through, remove from heat and stir in cooked peas. Season to taste with salt; sprinkle with lemon juice. Cover and refrigerate until chilled.   *Makes 6 servings.*

BREADFRUIT SALAD

Lovers of American potato salad can feel at home with this recipe, yet the breadfruit brings its own qualities that no potato possesses. Once you've tasted this, you just might switch your July 4th salad from all-American to à la Caribe.

1 medium breadfruit (about 2 pounds)
2 hard-cooked eggs
1 large onion, diced
1 large green bell pepper, diced
2 Scotch Bonnet or jalapeño chile slices, diced
1 cup diced, peeled, cooked shrimp or lobster, if desired
1/2 teaspoon ground white pepper
1/2 teaspoon salt
1/4 teaspoon garlic powder
1-1/2 to 2 cups mayonnaise
1 tablespoon vinegar
1/2 teaspoon prepared mustard

Preheat oven to 350F (175C). Place breadfruit in a roasting pan. Roast in preheated oven about 45 minutes or until soft when pierced with a skewer or knife. Cool, peel and dice breadfruit. Place in a large bowl. Chop eggs and add to breadfruit. Add diced onions, pepper, chile and shrimp if desired. Season with white pepper, salt and garlic powder. Add mayonnaise, vinegar and mustard, tossing until all ingredients are thoroughly blended. Cover and refrigerate until chilled.   *Makes 6 to 8 servings*.

PATTIES

These spicy meat pies originally hail from Haiti and now turn up delightfully on island after island. They are, deservedly, one of the most popular dishes in Caribbean restaurants in the United States.

2 cups all-purpose flour
1/2 tablespoon Curry Powder (page 27), or favorite commercial curry
    powder
1/2 teaspoon salt
1/2 cup vegetable shortening or margarine
Ice water
1 onion
2 green onions
1 Scotch Bonnet or jalapeño chile, seeds removed
3/4 pound ground beef
3 tablespoons vegetable oil
3/4 cup unseasoned dry bread crumbs
1/2 teaspoon dried leaf thyme
1 teaspoon Curry Powder, or favorite commercial curry powder
Salt and freshly ground black pepper to taste
1/2 cup water

To prepare pastry, sift together flour, 1/2 tablespoon Curry Powder and salt, then cut in shortening until mixture resembles peas. Add enough ice water to hold dough together. Wrap dough in plastic wrap and refrigerate at least 12 hours.

To make filling, finely chop onion, green onions and chile, then mix these seasonings thoroughly with ground beef. Heat oil in a skillet. Add meat mixture; cook until browned, about 10 minutes. Stir in bread crumbs, thyme, 1 teaspoon Curry Powder, salt and pepper. Mix filling well in pan, then add 1/2 cup water. Cover and simmer about 30 minutes. Cool filling.

Take dough out of refrigerator 15 minutes before using. Roll out to 1/4-inch thickness on a lightly floured board. Using a saucer for measurement, cut into 4-inch circles. Sprinkle a little flour on each circle before stacking and cover stack with a damp cloth.

Preheat oven to 400F (205C). Setting out the first pastry circle, top with 1/12th of filling to cover half of it. Fold other half over and seal edge by pressing down with a fork. Repeat with remaining filling and pastry circles. Place patties on 2 baking sheets. Bake in preheated oven 30 minutes, or until golden brown. *Makes about 12 patties.*

FRUIT SALAD

Fruit salad seems familiar enough; yet the tropical tastes in this one (not to mention the final sprinkle of coconut) go a long way toward making it island food.

2 ripe papayas
1/2 fresh pineapple
2 large bananas
1/4 pound green seedless grapes
3 tangerines or 2 oranges
Juice of 1 orange
Juice of 1 lemon
2 mint sprigs, coarsely chopped
2 tablespoons kirsch
2 tablespoons shredded coconut

Cut papayas in half, scoop out seeds and peel. Cut papayas into 1-inch cubes and place them in a large bowl. Remove pineapple top; peel and core, then cut it into 1-inch cubes and add to papaya. Peel bananas and slice them thinly. Halve grapes. Peel tangerines and remove white membrane, separating into sections. Add all these to bowl of fruit. Add orange and lemon juices, mint and kirsch. Toss well. Cover and refrigerate several hours before serving. Sprinkle with coconut and serve immediately. *Makes 6 servings.*

CRABMEAT SALAD

In the old days, crabmeat that had passed its prime was marinated for several hours in a dressing such as this to cover up its age. Today, with fresh lump crabmeat, it's simple to just mix and serve.

2 pounds cooked lump crabmeat, chilled
3 large tomatoes
3/4 cup freshly squeezed lime juice
2 garlic cloves, minced
1 cup Spanish-style green olives
1/2 cup thinly sliced green onions
Salt and freshly ground black pepper to taste
6 large iceberg or butter lettuce leaves
6 lime halves

Break crabmeat into large attractive chunks. Remove any shell or cartilage. Core and coarsely dice tomatoes, then combine them in a large bowl with lime juice, garlic, olives, green onions and crabmeat. Gently mix all ingredients together and season to taste with salt and pepper. To serve, place a lettuce leaf on each of 6 plates and spoon equal portions of crabmeat mixture onto each plate. Garnish with lime halves.   *Makes 6 servings.*

CRAB CLAWS

If you're preparing a dish that uses every tasty part of the crab except the claws, do not despair. Save the claws for this French-influenced island appetizer.

18 cooked crab claws
1 small onion, sliced
2 tomatoes, thinly sliced
2 tablespoons red wine vinegar
1/4 cup olive oil
1 tablespoon vegetable oil
Salt and freshly ground black pepper to taste
3 tablespoons chopped fresh basil

Arrange crab claws on a large platter with onion and tomatoes. In a small bowl, mix together vinegar, oils, salt and pepper. Spoon dressing over crab claws, onion and tomatoes, then sprinkle with chopped basil. *Makes 6 servings.*

LOBSTER SALAD

Lobster salads are always popular around the French West Indies, where the blend of simplicity and sophistication strikes just the right chord. This recipes comes from Guadeloupe.

2 teaspoons fresh lime juice
2 tablespoons olive oil
1 garlic clove, minced
Salt and freshly ground black pepper to taste
1 large onion, chopped
2-1/2 cups minced lobster meat (about 1 [1-1/2-lb.] cooked lobster)
Lettuce leaves
Avocado slices tossed with lemon juice
Ripe olives

In a small bowl, mix lime juice, olive oil, garlic, salt and pepper. Combine onion and lobster in a medium bowl. Add dressing, toss gently, cover and refrigerate at least 1 hour. To serve, arrange lettuce leaves on 6 salad plates. Divide lobster salad among lettuce leaves. Garnish with avocado slices and ripe olives. *Makes 6 servings.*

EGGS STUFFED WITH CRABMEAT

Stuffed, or deviled, eggs are not only the province of the great American picnic. They turn up in the islands too, most often as a way of showcasing surplus meat when the crabs are really "running."

1/2 cup crabmeat
6 hard-cooked eggs
1/2 stalk celery, finely chopped
1 tablespoon mayonnaise
1/4 teaspoon chopped garlic
1/4 teaspoon chopped parsley
1 pinch of salt
Freshly ground black pepper to taste
1 teaspoon dry mustard
Hot pepper sauce to taste

Shred crabmeat; discard any shells or cartilage. Peel eggs and cut them in half lengthwise. Remove yolks and mash these thoroughly in a medium bowl; set whites aside. Add remaining ingredients and mix well. Stuff each egg half with filling. Cover and refrigerate until chilled before serving. *Makes 6 servings.*

CONCH FRITTERS

Americans tend to be suspicious of conch, even when encountered on their own national turf in the Florida Keys. The fact is that when it is prepared properly, conch can be a real treat. Here is the best recipe for Conch Fritters I've ever tasted, and it works with peeled shrimp or crabmeat as well.

1/2 pound conch meat
1/4 cup chopped green bell pepper
1/2 stalk celery, chopped
1/4 cup chopped onion
1 tablespoon tomato paste
1 tablespoon lemon juice
Red (cayenne) pepper to taste
1 cup all-purpose flour
About 1/2 cup water
Vegetable oil for deep-frying
Cocktail sauce or salsa

Rinse conch meat to remove grit. Pat dry. Grind conch. Mix ground conch, bell pepper, celery and onion, then add tomato paste, lemon juice and cayenne. Let sit about 10 minutes so flavors can blend, then stir in flour. Stir in enough water to make a stiff batter.

Heat oil in a deep-fryer until a dollop of cool conch batter floats to surface. One or two at a time, place 1-tablespoon portions of mixture in hot oil, letting each fritter cook until it is golden brown. If it does not turn in oil by itself, turn it until color is even. Drain fritters on a tray lined with paper towels. Serve hot as an appetizer (2 fritters per person) with your favorite cocktail sauce. *Makes 6 servings*.

VARIATION

Substitute 1 pound chopped, peeled shrimp for conch. Add 1/2 cup water. Cook as above.

Smoked Marlin Salad

Here's a dish you'll eat often if you attend the legendary billfish tournament held each autumn in Port Antonio on the north coast of Jamaica. The festive affair is sometimes almost as wild as the running of the bulls in Pamplona, except that fish stories carry the day.

2 pounds smoked marlin, or other smoked fish
6 cups mixed salad greens, cut in bite-size pieces
2 cups green peas, cooked, drained
1 cup julienned Swiss cheese (about 4 oz.)
1 red onion, cut in rings
1/2 cup mayonnaise
2 teaspoons sugar
Salt and freshly ground black pepper to taste
4 bacon slices, cooked, crumbled
Cherry tomatoes

Remove and discard all skin and bones from fish, then break flesh into flakes. In a large bowl, combine salad greens, peas, cheese, onion and fish. Cover and refrigerate until thoroughly chilled. To serve, combine mayonnaise and sugar in a small bowl, then season to taste with salt and black pepper. Pour dressing over salad and toss lightly. Sprinkle with crumbled bacon and cherry tomatoes. *Makes 6 servings.*

Hot Pepper Coconut

Few dishes are easier to make than this appetizer, known on Martinique as *souskai*.

1/2 coconut, peeled
1 teaspoon salt
1 garlic clove, minced
1 Scotch Bonnet or jalapeño chile, minced
Juice of 2 limes

With a potato peeler, cut coconut meat into long thin strips; set aside. Combine salt, garlic, chile and lime juice in a medium bowl. Add coconut strips; marinate 1 hour. Serve coconut in its marinade.   *Makes 6 servings.*

LIMBO CAKES

These little nibbles borrow the double-frying method the French discovered to puff out their souffle potatoes. Yet the green plantains contribute the island color and quirkiness embodied by the limbo.

3 or 4 large green plantains
4 cups salted water
2 cups vegetable oil
Salt

Peel plantains and slice them into 2-inch rounds, then soak slices in salted water about 30 minutes to remove some of the starchy flavor. Drain slices and pat dry with paper towels.

Heat oil in a deep heavy saucepan to 375F (190C) or until a 1-inch bread cube turns golden brown in 50 seconds. Add plantains; cook about 5 minutes, turning them once. Do not brown. Drain on paper towels. On waxed paper, flatten each slice to 1/2 inch thick with a rolling pin or the flat side of a mallet. Return slices to hot oil; fry until crisp and brown. Drain on paper towels and sprinkle with salt. *Makes 6 servings.*

ENID DONALDSON'S CHICKEN ROLL

Enid Donaldson is sometimes called the "Julia Child of Jamaica" for her cooking demonstrations on island television. She is also a delightful hostess, serving these lovely chicken roll-ups in her breezy Kingston home.

2 tablespoons margarine
1 onion, chopped
4 day-old white bread slices, crumbled
1-1/2 teaspoons salt
1/2 teaspoon freshly ground black pepper
6 deboned chicken breast halves
1 teaspoon sugar
2 teaspoons Pickapeppa Sauce
2 hard-cooked eggs, chopped

Preheat oven to 350F (175C). Melt margarine in a medium skillet over medium heat. Add onion; cook until softened. Add bread crumbs, 1/2 teaspoon of the salt and the black pepper. Mix thoroughly, then cool.

Pound chicken breast halves with flat side of a mallet, being careful not to break up meat, then season with remaining salt, pepper to taste, sugar and Pickapeppa Sauce. Cover each breast with a thin layer of stuffing and chopped eggs, roll carefully and secure with a wooden pick. Place rolls in a baking pan. Bake in preheated oven 1-1/2 hours. Cool and slice into bite-size pieces. *Makes 6 servings.*

RICE SALAD

This salad, popular in summertime on any island with an Indian influence, tastes as pungent as its colorful looks. And since it wears its spices on its sleeve, so to speak, it's a strong argument for mixing your own curry powder instead of using that indecipherable melange from a jar.

1/3 cup plain yogurt
1 tablespoon raisins
1 tablespoon minced onion
1 teaspoon Curry Powder (page 27), or favorite commercial curry powder
1 pinch of salt
1/8 teaspoon freshly ground black pepper
1/8 teaspoon turmeric
2 teaspoons cider vinegar
1 cup white rice, cooked, cooled
1/4 cup coarsely chopped green bell pepper
1/4 cup coarsely chopped red bell pepper
Lettuce leaves

In a medium-size bowl, combine yogurt, raisins, onion, Curry Powder, salt, black pepper, turmeric and vinegar. Stir in rice and bell peppers. Cover and refrigerate until chilled. Line 6 salad plates with lettuce leaves. Divide salad among plates. *Makes 6 servings*.

CURRIED CASHEW NUTS

Even cashews can go Caribbean, especially since they're actually the seed of a fruit that's native to the American tropics. Though the nut is most familiar in the United States, the tart fruit can be made into a cooling island drink, a perfumed preserve, vinegar and even wine.

1/4 cup butter or margarine
3 cups cashew nuts
1 teaspoon salt
2 teaspoons Curry Powder (page 27), or favorite commercial curry powder

Melt butter in a medium skillet over medium heat. Add cashews. Cook until lightly toasted. Drain on paper towels. Sprinkle with salt and Curry Powder. *Makes 3 cups.*

Solomon Gundy

This dish, sometimes called salamagundy, harks back to English colonial days on Jamaica and Barbados. It clearly is an effort to spice up the salted fish that appeared so often on spartan island tables. Yet even today, it makes an exotic and flavorful appetizer.

3/4 pound salt herring or other salted fish
1/3 cup vinegar
2 teaspoons minced onion
8 allspice berries
2 tablespoons vegetable oil
30 (1-1/2-inch) bread rounds
Butter
Paprika
Chopped parsley

Soak salt herring, or other salt fish, in enough water to cover in the refrigerator 8 hours, then drain, rinse and debone. Cut fish in 1/2-inch squares, place in a medium bowl and set aside. In a small saucepan, combine vinegar, onion and allspice. Boil 1 minute, then remove from heat and add oil. Pour this liquid over reserved fish squares and marinate, covered, in refrigerator 24 hours. To serve, toast bread rounds and spread with butter. Drain fish and top each toast round with a square. Garnish with paprika and chopped parsley. *Makes 30 appetizers.*

PEPPER SHRIMP

When you see bandannaed ladies on the side of the road selling bright orange somethings in clear little bags, this is what they're selling. Pepper shrimp are a favorite nibble all along the coast of Jamaica.

5 pounds shrimp, in the shell
1 cup vegetable oil
2 cloves garlic, minced
2 teaspoons salt
2 Scotch Bonnet chiles, minced
2 tablespoons vinegar

Heat the oil, garlic, salt and pepper in a heavy Dutch oven, then add the shrimp and stir for 5 minutes. Sprinkle on the vinegar and stir for 5 more minutes. *Makes 6 to 8 servings.*

CALLALOO QUICHE

The delicious island green called *callaloo* provides just the touch to turn a European dish into a Caribbean classic. This recipe is served with great success at Good Hope Great House.

4 ounces (1 cup) shredded Cheddar cheese
1 (9-inch) Pie Crust (page 182), unbaked
1 medium onion, chopped
1 tablespoon unsalted butter
3 eggs, beaten
2 cups milk
3/4 pound chopped callaloo, cooked
1/2 teaspoon salt
1 dash of freshly ground black pepper
2 Scotch Bonnet chiles, chopped

Preheat the oven to 425F (230C). Sprinkle 1/2 of the cheese in the crust. Melt the butter in a small skillet over medium heat. Add onion and sauté until tender, then mix in the eggs, milk, callaloo, salt, pepper and chiles.

Carefully pour over cheese in crust. Sprinkle the remaining cheese over the top and bake 30 to 35 minutes, until a knife inserted in the center comes out clean. *Makes 6 to 8 servings.*

Steamed Callaloo in Phyllo Dough

As an example of what young chefs in Jamaica are doing today, here's a starter that uses both callaloo and ackee—but in a creative, New World sort of way. This dish is a favorite at the San Souci all-inclusive resort in Ocho Rios.

1 tablespoon butter
1/2 teaspoon minced garlic
1 small onion, minced
1/4 teaspoon minced fresh thyme
1/2 Scotch Bonnet chile, minced
2 pounds callaloo leaves, rinsed and chopped
2 medium tomatoes, diced
10 ounces shredded (2-1/2 cups) mild Cheddar cheese
8 sheets phyllo dough
Vegetable oil for brushing

Ackee Sauce

10 white peppercorns
1 bay leaf
1/2 cup white wine
6 cups whipping cream
12 ounces ackee, cooked, squeezed of all water and pureed
9 ounces unsalted butter, cut into pieces
Salt and freshly ground pepper

Melt butter in a skillet. Add garlic, onion, thyme and chile and sauté until softened. Add the callaloo and tomatoes. Cook, stirring, over medium heat 5 to 7 minutes or until tender. Season with salt and pepper and allow to cool, then add the cheese.

Lay out the phyllo, one sheet at a time, brushing with a little vegetable oil and folding in half. Place 1/8 of the callaloo mixture in the middle of the sheet and fold the phyllo in a neat package. Brush the top with a little more oil. Repeat this procedure 8 times. Place on an ungreased baking sheet.

Preheat the oven to 350F (175C). Prepare the sauce. Bake the phyllo packages until golden brown, about 10 minutes. Serve immediately with the sauce. *Makes 8 servings.*

ACKEE SAUCE

Place the peppercorns and bay leaf in a heavy saucepan, cover with white wine and bring to a boil. Reduce until almost dry, then strain the reduction into a clean saucepan. Add the cream and cook until reduced to 2 cups. Add the pureed ackee and simmer 1 minute. Remove from the heat and whisk in the butter, one piece at a time. Season with salt and pepper.

Soups

A visitor from the north, basking in the winter sunshine and the warm trade winds, might not think of soup as the perfect Caribbean nourishment. Indeed, he might guess that the Caribbean people never eat soup at all. But the visitor would not only be incorrect but he'd miss out on some of the best food the islands have to offer.

From the earliest habitation by Indians from South America, soup has staked its claim as one of the most traditional island foods. Just about every island cook has a favorite home-made soup. As in other parts of the world, soup's basic simplicity and versatility make it the perfect showcase for whatever is fresh and available. Whether the island be rich in seafood or enjoy enough space and fertile soil to grow terrific vegetables, you will find these wonders in the local soups.

TOMATO & PEANUT SOUP

Any Caribbean recipe using peanuts can be subtitled "Out of Africa." Peanuts, or ground nuts (as they're still sometimes called), came over with the slaves. This soup is especially loved by the islands' Creoles.

2 tablespoons vegetable oil
2 onions, minced
2 tablespoons all-purpose flour
3 cups milk
1/2 cup smooth peanut butter
1 teaspoon celery salt
Freshly ground black pepper to taste
3 cups tomato juice

Heat oil in a large saucepan. Add onions; cook until soft but not brown. Add flour and stir 2 minutes over low heat. Remove saucepan from heat. In a medium bowl, stir milk slowly into peanut butter until mixture is smooth. Add celery salt and pepper. Stir milk mixture slowly into onion mixture. Return pan to medium heat and cook, stirring often, until liquid thickens. Do not boil. Stir in tomato juice and refrigerate at least 1 hour before serving. *Makes 6 servings.*

Papaya & Garlic Soup

Papaya and garlic might seem an unusual combination if you've never encountered it. But once you have, either in this soup or in Sautéed Shrimp with Roasted Garlic & Papaya, you'll see what you've been missing.

4 cups Chicken Stock (page 23)
3 cups chopped papaya pulp (3 to 4 papayas)
8 garlic cloves
1/2 pint (1 cup) whipping cream
Salt and freshly ground black pepper

In a large pot, mix stock, papaya and garlic; bring to a boil. Reduce heat and simmer 45 minutes. Add cream and heat through, then season to taste with salt and pepper. Puree in a blender or food processor fitted with the steel blade. Return soup to pan and reheat. If it seems too thick, add more stock. Serve immediately. *Makes 6 servings.*

Turtle Soup

Turtle meat is getting easier to find in the United States, a definite boon since few American cooks voluntarily take on a whole live turtle. Like conch, turtle tends to be tough, but the lengthy cooking favored in the Caribbean solves this problem.

3 pounds turtle meat, cubed
1 small smoked ham hock
3 green onions, finely chopped
1 celery stalk, finely chopped
1 bay leaf
1 teaspoon minced parsley
3 quarts water
3 tomatoes, chopped
1 thyme sprig
12 allspice berries
1 or 2 Scotch Bonnet or jalapeño chiles, sliced lengthwise
Salt and freshly ground black pepper to taste

Place turtle meat, ham hock, green onions, celery, bay leaf and parsley in a large pot. Pour in the water and bring to a boil, then reduce heat and simmer until meats are tender, about 1-1/2 hours. Add tomatoes, thyme, allspice berries, chile, salt and black pepper. Add more water if necessary. Simmer soup another 5 minutes, then remove bay leaf and thyme. *Makes 6 servings.*

CONCH SOUP

This lovely soup pairs the ever-popular conch with the chayote. Slow cooking is the key.

3 pounds conch meat, thawed if frozen
Juice of 2 limes
3 quarts water
1 chayote, diced
4 potatoes, cubed
2 thyme sprigs
3 green onions, finely chopped
2 Scotch Bonnet or jalapeño chiles, finely chopped
Salt and freshly ground black pepper to taste

Rinse any grit from conch and pat dry, then squeeze lime juice over meat and rub it in with your fingers. Cut conch into small cubes. Bring water and conch to a boil in a medium saucepan. Reduce heat, cover and simmer until tender, about 2 hours. When conch is tender, add chayote, potatoes, thyme, green onions and chiles. Season to taste with salt and black pepper. Bring to a boil, then reduce heat and simmer until vegetables are tender. *Makes 6 servings.*

VARIATION

Substitute chopped clams for conch.

TURKEY & OKRA SOUP

If you're tired of endless turkey sandwiches after Thanksgiving, you might try this idea from chefs in the Caribbean. Turkey stock is a revelation unto itself, and the okra as always adds both flavor and thickening.

2 cups all-purpose flour
1 tablespoon vegetable shortening
1 cup water
2 egg yolks
Salt and freshly ground black pepper to taste
1 tablespoon butter or margarine
2 pounds cooked turkey meat, cut into small pieces
1 green bell pepper, diced
1 medium onion, diced
1 medium tomato, chopped
1 garlic clove, finely chopped
1 or 2 Scotch Bonnet or jalapeño chiles, chopped
2 quarts Turkey Stock (page 22)
1/2 pound fresh okra, cut crosswise in 1-inch slices

Prepare a dumpling batter: mix together flour, shortening, water and egg yolks in a medium bowl. Season with salt and black pepper. Set aside. Melt butter in large pot. Add turkey; cook 2 minutes, then add bell pepper, onion, tomato, garlic and chile. Sauté 3 minutes, then pour in stock and simmer 30 minutes. Add okra and cook 20 minutes, until it is crisp-tender. Drop reserved batter by teaspoonfuls into hot liquid to make dumplings the size of nickels. Simmer, uncovered, 5 to 10 minutes, or until dumplings are done. Season to taste with salt and pepper. *Makes 6 servings.*

SHRIMP & BANANA BROTH

Underripe bananas behave more like a starchy vegetable than fruit in this promising pairing with shrimp. The Pickapeppa Sauce is a pungent after-thought.

7 small green bananas
1 pound shrimp, peeled, deveined
1-1/2 teaspoons salt
1 large tomato, peeled, seeded, diced
1 onion, chopped
2 Scotch Bonnet or jalapeño chiles, finely chopped
1 thyme sprig
4 teaspoons Pickapeppa Sauce

Peel 4 of the bananas, leaving remaining 3 unpeeled. Cut peeled bananas in half crosswise. Bring 1-1/2 quarts water to a boil, add shrimp and salt and boil 2 to 3 minutes. Add peeled bananas, tomato, onion, chiles, thyme and Pickapeppa Sauce. Cook over medium heat 15 to 20 minutes. When soup is ready to serve, peel remaining bananas; cut in half crosswise. Place 2 pieces of banana in each cup. Spoon soup over bananas. *Makes 6 servings.*

HOT BANANA SOUP

The mixing of starchy vegetables and stock for soup is nothing out of the ordinary; the addition of rum, chile and coconut carries this recipe straight to the islands.

12 green bananas
1 quart Beef Stock (page 24)
1 jigger light rum
2 tablespoons vegetable oil
1 green onion, finely chopped
1 Scotch Bonnet or jalapeño chile, finely chopped
1 cup grated fresh coconut
Croutons

Peel and mash bananas, then mix them with stock and pass mixture through a sieve into a medium bowl. Add rum. Heat oil in a large saucepan. Add green onion, chile and coconut; cook, stirring, until softened. Pour in strained banana-beef stock; cook over medium heat until bananas are tender, about 30 minutes. Serve piping hot with croutons.   *Makes 6 servings.*

CORN CHOWDER

Yellow corn, often called maize or Indian corn in the Caribbean, goes back to the days of the Arawaks—as, I'm certain, does some variation on this chowder.

4 ounces salt pork, diced
1 small onion, diced
1 celery stalk, diced
2 medium boiling potatoes, cubed
2-1/2 cups water
1/2 teaspoon sugar
1/2 teaspoon salt
1/4 teaspoon freshly ground black pepper
2-1/2 cups milk
4 ears of corn, cooked, cut off (about 2 cups)
Paprika

Sauté salt pork in a large kettle until it is lightly browned and crisp. Add onion and celery; cook until tender but not browned. Add potatoes, the water, sugar, salt and black pepper. Cover and simmer until potatoes are tender. Add milk and corn; bring to a boil. Serve in warm bowls with a sprinkle of paprika for color. *Makes 6 servings.*

ANTILLES PEA SOUP

The Dutch battled the Spanish for longer than seems practical these days—thus the Eighty Year War from 1568 to 1648. But they never lost their taste for a Spanish soup made with split peas, even exporting it to their own islands in the Caribbean.

2 cups dried split peas
1 smoked ham hock
2 onions, coarsely chopped
2 carrots, coarsely chopped
1 celery stalk with leaves
1 garlic clove, crushed
1 bay leaf
1/2 teaspoon crushed rosemary
1 Scotch Bonnet or jalapeño chile
1/2 pound smoked sausage, sliced

Wash split peas thoroughly. Place in a medium bowl and cover with several inches cold water. Soak overnight. Drain, reserving liquid. Pour this liquid into a large pot; add all ingredients except soaked peas and sausage. Bring liquid to a boil, reduce heat and simmer 45 minutes. Strain broth, discarding vegetables, then skim off fat. Return broth and ham hock to heat; add soaked peas. Simmer 3 hours, or until peas are tender. Strain out peas; puree them in a food processor fitted with the steel blade, then return to soup. Add smoked sausage and heat thoroughly before serving. *Makes 6 to 8 servings.*

CALLALOO & IRISH POTATO SOUP

Regular potatoes are known as Irish potatoes in most of the Caribbean, presumably to distinguish them from sweet potatoes and a variety of other tubers. This hearty soup mixes them with fresh callaloo.

2 quarts water
2 small smoked ham hocks
1/2 pound beef short ribs
1 teaspoon salt
2 medium baking potatoes, diced
1-1/2 pounds callaloo or kale, chopped
3 tablespoons bacon drippings
1/2 medium onion, chopped
1/2 green bell pepper, chopped
1 Scotch Bonnet or jalapeño chile, chopped

Pour water into a large pot; add ham hocks, short ribs and salt. Bring to a boil; remove foam with a skimmer or spoon. Reduce heat and simmer 30 minutes, then add potatoes and callaloo. Meanwhile, in a medium skillet, heat bacon drippings; add onion and bell pepper. Cook until onion is transparent. Add to soup with chile. Bring to a boil and cook, uncovered, 10 minutes, then cover pot and cook until potatoes are done. *Makes 6 servings*.

Pepperpot

As far back as the first recipe swap between the Arawak Indians and their Spanish conquerors, the soup or stew called Pepperpot was so old no one knew where it came from. It remains the Caribbean's most famous soup.

2 pounds fresh kale
1/2 pound callaloo, or spinach
12 okra pods
1/4 pound salt pork, cut into thin strips
1/2 pound lean fresh pork, cubed
2 onions, thinly sliced
Freshly ground black pepper to taste
1 Scotch Bonnet or jalapeño chile, seeds removed, sliced
1 tablespoon chopped fresh thyme or 1 teaspoon dried leaf thyme
6 cups Chicken Stock (page 23)

Pull all stems from kale and callaloo. Discard stems and roughly chop leaves. Wash leaves thoroughly. Roughly chop okra. Place salt pork in a large, heavy soup kettle; sauté over medium heat 10 minutes, rendering out fat. Discard all but 2 tablespoons of fat. Add pork cubes and onions to pan; sauté over medium heat until cubes are brown and onions are translucent, about 5 minutes. Add kale, callaloo, okra, black pepper and chile. Add thyme and stock. Cover and simmer 2-1/2 hours. Remove salt pork before serving. *Makes 6 to 8 servings.*

BLACK BEAN SOUP

Here is a delicious Cuban soup that can be made ahead and refrigerated or frozen. In fact, I like to double the recipe and freeze half for another meal.

1/2 pound dried black beans
4 cups water
4 cups Beef Stock (page 24)
1 smoked ham hock or 4-ounce piece smoked ham
1/4 cup dry sherry
Salt and freshly ground black pepper to taste
3 cups hot cooked rice
1/2 cup chopped green onions
1/2 cup chopped cooked ham

Rinse and sort beans. Place in a medium bowl and cover with several inches of cold water. Soak overnight. Drain beans; place them in a large pot. Add the 4 cups water, stock and ham, then simmer 2 hours, or until beans are tender. Remove ham hock and let it cool just enough to handle. Chop meat into small chunks and discard skin and bones. In a blender or food processor fitted with the steel blade, puree half of the beans. Return pureed beans to pot along with ham hock chunks and sherry. Reheat gently and season to taste with salt and pepper. Serve with rice. Pass green onions and chopped ham separately. *Makes 6 servings.*

YAM BISQUE

The islands' best cooks have a knack for making dishes seem traditional and innovative at the same time. This yam bisque is a delightful example.

4 cups diced yams (about 2 pounds)
1 cup water
3 tablespoons butter or margarine
3 tablespoons finely chopped onion
3 cups Fish Stock (page 25) or Chicken Stock (page 23)
3 cups milk
1/2 teaspoon sugar
1/2 teaspoon salt
1/2 teaspoon white pepper
2 teaspoons lime juice
1/2 pint (1 cup) whipping cream

Place diced yams in a large saucepan with the water; boil 20 minutes, until tender. Drain yams, discarding water. In a separate saucepan, melt butter. Add onion; cook until softened. Add boiled yams, followed by stock, milk, sugar, salt and white pepper. Stir well, then bring to a boil. Add lime juice. Simmer 30 minutes. Press soup through a sieve, forcing through as much of the yams as possible. Heat cream in a separate saucepan (do not let it boil), then add it to strained soup. Mix well. Serve hot. *Makes 6 servings*.

Pumpkin Soup

Next time you decide to make pumpkin soup during the holidays, try it à la Caribe. This soup packs a good bit more punch than the one appearing on most American tables.

2 pounds beef shanks
1/2 pound pig's tail
2 pounds pumpkin, peeled, cubed
1/2 pound yams, peeled, cubed
1 thyme sprig, finely chopped
1 whole Scotch Bonnet or jalapeño chile
1 garlic clove, minced
Grated gingerroot to taste
Salt and freshly ground black pepper to taste

Place beef shanks and pig's tail in 4 quarts water in a large pot. Boil until almost tender, about 1 hour. Add pumpkin, yams, thyme, chile and garlic; boil until pumpkin and yams are soft. Discard cooked meats. Remove pumpkin and yams; crush and return to pot. Remove chile and discard. Add gingerroot to taste, then season with salt and black pepper. *Makes 6 servings.*

CHILLED PAPAYA SOUP

It seems that many Americans are just realizing the summer joys of cold fruit soups. Papaya turns up in most supermarkets now, and this preparation is all tropics.

3 medium papayas
1-1/2 cups water
About 1/3 cup freshly squeezed lime juice
1/2 cup brandy

Peel papayas and cut a portion of 1 into 20 to 24 small cubes. Set these aside and place remaining papayas in a blender, add water and puree. Pour pureed papaya mixture into a medium bowl; add lime juice in small amounts, stopping when it suits your taste. Whisk in brandy, cover and refrigerate 1 hour. To serve, place reserved papaya cubes in individual cups and pour soup over cubes. For an elegant touch, pour 1 teaspoon of lighted brandy over each bowl of soup when served. *Makes 6 servings.*

COLD MANGO SOUP LACED WITH RUM

Like papayas, mangoes are becoming refreshingly common in American markets. This cold soup is the best one using mango that I've discovered.

5 mangoes
1 cup sugar
5 cups Chicken Stock (page 23)
1/4 teaspoon ground cinnamon
1 or 2 whole cloves
1/4 teaspoon ground ginger
2 tablespoons rum
1/2 cup whipping cream
Freshly grated nutmeg, if desired

Peel, seed and chop mangoes, then place them with the rest of the ingredients except rum, whipped cream and nutmeg in a heavy saucepan. Cook over medium heat; skim any foam from top. Reduce until about 1/4 of original liquid has evaporated, then press mixture through a sieve. Cover and refrigerate at least 1 hour. Add rum immediately before serving. Whip cream in a small bowl. Top each serving with whipped cream and nutmeg, if desired. *Makes 6 servings.*

Coconut Soup

Coconut is such a wonderful extra touch in so many Caribbean dishes, it's interesting now and again to give it the starring role.

3 cups freshly grated coconut
5 cups Chicken Stock (page 23)
2 tablespoons butter, softened
2 tablespoons all-purpose flour
1/2 cup whipping cream
Salt and white pepper to taste

In a large heavy saucepan, combine coconut and stock; bring to a boil. Reduce heat and simmer, covered, 30 minutes. Strain hot mixture through a sieve, squeezing coconut with the back of a spoon to extract all its liquid. Discard coconut. In a large bowl, cream together butter and flour, adding coconut liquid a little at a time and stirring constantly to make a smooth consistency. Place new mixture in saucepan and cook over medium-high heat until thickened, about 5 minutes. Remove from heat; stir in whipping cream. Season to taste with salt and white pepper. *Makes 6 servings.*

CHIP-CHIP CHOWDER

It's worth cooking this Trinidadian favorite just to lovingly pronounce its name. Actually, chip-chips are tiny shellfish whose best substitutes are little-neck clams. Unlike New England clam chowder, this one uses no cream and unlike Manhattan clam chowder, it uses no tomatoes.

4 dozen clams
4 cups water
Chicken broth
1 pound potatoes, peeled and diced
1 large onion, chopped
2 green onions, chopped
1 teaspoon minced fresh thyme
1 Scotch Bonnet chile (whole)
2 tablespoons butter
1 tablespoon freshly squeezed lime juice
Minced cilantro

Wash the clams and set them in a large pot, add the water and cook over medium heat until the shells open. Discard any unopened clams. Remove the clam meat from the shells and discard the necks. Reserve the clam meat.

Strain the broth through muslin and combine with enough chicken broth to make 6 cups. Return the liquid to the pot and add the potatoes, onion, green onion, thyme and chile. Cook over medium heat 30 minutes. Remove the chile. Strain the broth, reserving vegetables.

Puree the vegetables in a food processor, then return the puree and liquid in the pot. Add the clam meat, butter and lime juice. Simmer 5 to 10 minutes, until the mixture thickens. Garnish with minced cilantro and serve. *Makes 6 servings.*

RED PEA SOUP WITH SPINNERS

In yet another use of Jamaica's omnipresent kidney bean (red peas), here's a delightful soup that has just enough heat to lift it above similar soups elsewhere.

The spinners are dense dumplings that are cooked on the soup.

1-1/2 pounds beef stew meat, cut into cubes
3/4 pound pig's tail or ham, chopped
2 cups dried kidney beans, soaked overnight and drained
4 quarts water
2 Scotch Bonnet chiles (whole)
1 sprig fresh thyme
1/2 pound potato or yellow yam
3 green onions
Salt to taste

SPINNERS

1 cup all-purpose flour
1 pinch of salt
About 1/3 cup water

Place meats, kidney beans and water in a large pot over medium heat. Bring to a boil. Reduce heat and simmer, covered, about 2 hours, or until the beans are soft. Add the chiles, thyme, potato and green onions. Simmer 30 minutes or until potato is almost tender.

Prepare spinners and place on top of soup. Cover and cook 15 minutes. Discard chile. Serve hot. *Makes 6 servings*.

SPINNERS

Mix together flour, salt and enough water to make a stiff dough. Pinch off walnut-size balls. In the palm of your hands, knead and shape into long, thin dumplings. Add to the soup during last 15 minutes of cooking.

BEEF SOUP

Traditionally, cows in the Caribbean were slaughtered on Friday. Since the bones spoiled quickly in the heat, they were quickly turned into soup—giving this home-style recipe the alternate name "Saturday Soup."

1 pound beef soup bones
2 quarts water
1/2 pound carrots, cubed
1/4 pound turnips, cubed
1 pound pumpkin meat, cut up
1/2 pound chayote, cubed
1 pound yellow yam, cubed
1/2 pound cabbage
1 sprig fresh thyme
2 green onions

Boil the bones in the water in a large pot over medium heat 1 hour. Add remaining ingredients. Bring to a boil, then simmer, uncovered, until the yam is cooked, about 40 minutes, stirring occasionally. Cut any meat from bones and return to soup. Discard bones. Serve hot.   *Makes 6 servings.*

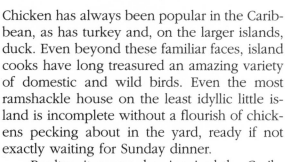

POULTRY

Chicken has always been popular in the Caribbean, as has turkey and, on the larger islands, duck. Even beyond these familiar faces, island cooks have long treasured an amazing variety of domestic and wild birds. Even the most ramshackle house on the least idyllic little island is incomplete without a flourish of chickens pecking about in the yard, ready if not exactly waiting for Sunday dinner.

Poultry, it seems, has inspired the Caribbean as far back as people remember their mothers' cooking—and that, as we know, is a very long time. Everyone has a beloved chicken stew deliciously spiked with hot chile peppers, and everyone has a favorite marinade or basting sauce for chicken served sizzling from the grill. It is in these marinades and sauces, in fact, that the Caribbean makes its part in the process known.

TANGY GRILLED CHICKEN

Islanders love to cook outdoors, just as Americans do. Yet most cooks in the Caribbean take it as a matter of pride to make their own spicy marinades rather than just open a bottle of barbecue sauce. This recipe presents one of the best tangy marinades I've found.

2 broiler-fryer chickens
2 tablespoons butter or margarine
2 garlic cloves, minced
2 shallots, minced
3 tablespoons tomato paste
1/2 cup dry white wine
1/4 cup wine vinegar
1 large green bell pepper, finely chopped
1 teaspoon dried leaf thyme
1 Scotch Bonnet or jalapeño chile, finely chopped
1 teaspoon Worcestershire sauce

Cut chicken into serving pieces. Melt butter in a medium saucepan. Add garlic and shallots; cook until lightly browned. Stir in tomato paste, followed by wine and vinegar. Add bell pepper, thyme, chile and Worcestershire sauce. Bring to a boil, reduce heat and simmer for 5 minutes. Cool to room temperature.

Place chicken in a large shallow pan and pour sauce on top. Marinate, covered, 2 to 3 hours in refrigerator. Preheat grill. Arrange chicken on hot grill and cook, turning pieces often and basting with sauce, about 20 minutes or until juices run clear when chicken is pierced with a knife. *Makes 6 to 8 servings.*

PEPPERY CHICKEN & RICE

It doesn't take a kitchen scholar to realize this dish began its life as Spanish *arroz con pollo*. Yet it never packed quite the punch in Madrid or Seville that it does in Cuba, Puerto Rico or the Dominican Republic.

2 black peppercorns
4 garlic cloves, chopped
1 teaspoon dried leaf oregano
2 teaspoons salt
1 Scotch Bonnet or jalapeño chile
3 tablespoons olive oil
1 teaspoon freshly squeezed lime juice
1 (3-lb.) chicken, cut in serving pieces
2 ounces lean ham, diced
1 ounce salt pork, diced
1 onion, chopped
1 red bell pepper, chopped
1 green bell pepper, chopped
1 cup uncooked rice
4 or 5 saffron threads, crushed
2 cups Chicken Stock (page 23)
Salt and freshly ground black pepper to taste
Lime wedges

Using a mortar and pestle, crush and mix peppercorns, 2 garlic cloves, oregano, salt, chile, 2 tablespoons olive oil and lime juice. Rinse and pat dry chicken pieces, then rub with seasoning mixture. Cover and refrigerate several hours, or preferably overnight.

In a large skillet, heat the remaining 1 tablespoon olive oil until hot. Add ham and salt pork; cook until browned. Reduce heat to medium and add chicken pieces, browning on all sides, about 5 minutes. Remove all meats; set aside. Reduce heat. Add onion, bell peppers and remaining garlic; cook until the onion is soft. Add rice and saffron, stirring constantly until the rice is thoroughly coated with oil. Pour stock into the skillet and stir, then place chicken, ham and salt pork on top of the rice-vegetable mixture. Cover and simmer until all the liquid is absorbed, about 30 minutes. Season to taste with salt and black pepper. Garnish with lime wedges. *Makes 6 servings.*

Bajan Fried Chicken

Natives of Barbados (who call themselves Bajans, no matter how many different variations travel writers dream up) love this fried chicken with fiery spices. It is a version of "seasoning up" as it's called on many islands. You might even prefer to refrigerate the chicken with the spices for an hour or two, to let the flavors really take hold.

1 (4-lb.) whole chicken
Seasoning Mix (see below)
Vegetable oil for deep-frying
1 cup all-purpose flour
Salt and freshly ground black pepper to taste
2 eggs, lightly beaten
3-1/2 cups unseasoned dry bread crumbs

Seasoning Mix

2 medium onions
2 parsley sprigs, chopped
1 tablespoon chopped fresh thyme
1 tablespoon chopped fresh marjoram
1 tablespoon chopped fresh chives
1/2 teaspoon ground cloves
2 garlic cloves, chopped
2 Scotch Bonnet or jalapeño chiles, chopped
1 teaspoon paprika
Juice of 1 lime
Salt to taste

Bring a large pot of salted water to a boil. Add chicken, then reduce heat, cover and simmer until chicken is tender, 30 to 40 minutes. Prepare Seasoning Mix. Drain chicken and pat it dry. Cool completely, then cut into 8 serving pieces. Cut a long, deep pocket in meaty part of each piece, filling each pocket with about 2 tablespoons of Seasoning Mix.

Heat oil in a deep-fryer or large skillet to 375F (190C) or until a 1-inch bread cube turns golden brown in 50 seconds. On a large plate, combine flour, salt and pepper; coat chicken pieces, shaking off any excess flour. Dip pieces into beaten eggs, then roll them in bread crumbs to coat thoroughly. Fry in batches (without crowding) until golden brown, 2 to 3 minutes on each side. Drain on paper towels. *Makes 4 servings.*

SEASONING MIX

Peel and coarsely chop onions. Place them with remaining ingredients in a blender or food processor fitted with the steel blade. Process 1 to 2 minutes, until fairly smooth. (This mixture can be spooned into a jar and refrigerated several weeks for use as needed.)

FRICASSEED CHICKEN

This is the typical islander's favorite way to cook and eat chicken, though the recipes vary so much it's hard to call it one dish. Well, it is a one-dish meal— and here's an excellent rendition that should help explain its popularity.

1 (2- to 3-lb.) chicken, cut in serving pieces
2 teaspoons salt
1 teaspoon sugar
1 teaspoon black pepper
1 Scotch Bonnet chile, chopped
4 garlic cloves, crushed
3 green onions, finely chopped
2 sprigs fresh thyme
2 tablespoons vegetable oil
2 cups chicken broth or water
1 tablespoon Pickapeppa Sauce
1-1/2 tablespoons ketchup
1/2 pound potatoes, peeled and chopped
1/4 pound carrots, chopped
1 medium chayote, chopped
2 large onions, chopped

Season the chicken with the salt, sugar, pepper, chile, garlic, green onions and thyme. Heat the oil in a large saucepan over medium heat. Add the chicken and cook until browned, turning. Add the broth or water, Pickapeppa Sauce and ketchup. Add the vegetables and simmer about 30 minutes, stirring occasionally, or until chicken and vegetables are tender. Serve hot. *Makes 6 servings*.

ROAST DUCK WITH LIME SAUCE

On the larger islands, wildfowl have been a part of the culinary melting pot for centuries. Even on the smaller islands, with the advances in fresh food shipment, they have become quite popular. Here is one of the best things islands cooks do with a nice fresh duck.

1 (6-pound) duck with neck and giblets
1 carrot, coarsely chopped
1 celery stalk with leaves, coarsely chopped
1 medium onion, coarsely chopped
Salt and freshly ground black pepper to taste
2 Scotch Bonnet or jalapeño chiles, finely chopped
1/2 teaspoon dried leaf thyme
2 limes
1/2 cup dry white wine
1/2 cup Chicken Stock (page 23)
1/4 cup sugar
3 tablespoons white wine vinegar
1 teaspoon cornstarch blended with 1 teaspoon water

Preheat oven to 375F (190C). Rinse duck and dry it thoroughly, then chop neck and giblets coarsely and place them in a large roasting pan. Add carrot, celery and onion. Sprinkle duck inside and out with salt, black pepper, chiles and thyme. With a fork, prick thighs and fat to allow fat to drain. Place duck in roasting pan breast-side down. Cook in preheated oven 30 minutes. Remove duck from pan and spoon or pour off fat, then set duck on its side and return it to oven. Roast 30 minutes. Again remove pan from oven and remove as much fat as you can.

Increase oven temperature to 400F (205C). Turn duck onto its other side and roast 30 minutes. Remove from oven and pour off fat, then turn duck breast-side up and roast 40 minutes.

Meanwhile, with a vegetable peeler, remove green outer peel of limes. Squeeze limes and set juice aside. Cut peel into julienne strips and drop these into a small saucepan of boiling water. Boil about 1 minute and drain. Place duck on a serving platter and keep it warm in turned-off oven while preparing sauce.

Pour off remaining fat from roasting pan, then place pan atop stove over medium heat and add white wine. Cook while stirring to loosen browned particles, then add stock. In another small saucepan, bring sugar and vinegar to a boil. Cook over high heat until mixture is lightly caramelized, watching carefully so it does not burn. Immediately pour vinegar mixture into pan with pan juices. Bring to a boil. Add 2 tablespoons of reserved lime juice along with cornstarch mixture. Cook until sauce returns to a boil. Season to taste with salt, pepper and additional lime juice. Stir in julienned lime peel. Carve duck and spoon hot lime sauce over it. *Makes 6 servings.*

CHICKEN WITH GINGER & TAMARIND

Ginger and tamarind are among the absolute favorite flavorings in the Caribbean, so it was only a matter of time before someone tried putting them together.

5 pounds chicken pieces
Juice of 1 lemon or lime
1/4 cup vegetable oil
3 garlic cloves, chopped
2 medium onions, chopped
1 tablespoon grated gingerroot
2 cups tamarind nectar
1 cup water
Salt and freshly ground black pepper to taste

Rinse and pat dry chicken, then rub it with lemon or lime juice. Heat oil in a large skillet over medium-high heat. Add chicken in batches; lightly brown chicken. Remove; set pieces aside. Reduce heat slightly and add garlic. Stir, then add onions; cook until lightly colored. Stir in gingerroot. Pour in tamarind nectar and water. Season to taste with salt and pepper. Return chicken pieces to skillet, bring to a boil, cover and reduce heat. Simmer 1 hour, until chicken is tender. *Makes 6 servings.*

Virgin Islands Breast of Duck

This recipe reflects the sophistication and innovation of chefs working in Charlotte Amalie, the shopping-crazed capital of the U.S. Virgin Islands.

4 (8-ounce) boneless duck breasts
Marinade, see below
Papaya Sauce, see below
3 tablespoons butter or margarine

Marinade

2 cups dry white wine
2 tablespoons chopped fresh basil
2 tablespoons chopped fresh parsley
1 lemon, quartered
Salt and freshly ground black pepper to taste

Papaya Sauce

3 cups peeled, seeded, diced papaya (about 1 large papaya)
1/4 cup lemon juice
1/2 cup dry white wine
Salt and freshly ground black pepper to taste
1 bay leaf
1/2 cup whipping cream
Cornstarch if needed to thicken

Make marinade. Add duck breasts to marinade, cover and refrigerate overnight or up to 3 or 4 days for the fullest flavor. When ready to serve, make Papaya Sauce.

Remove duck breasts from marinade and pat dry. Melt butter in a heavy skillet over medium-high heat. Add duck breasts; quickly cook in butter 2 to 3 minutes on each side. Do not overcook—duck should be served medium rare. Remove breasts from skillet and slice diagonally.

Cover bottom of 4 warmed dinner plates with sauce and top with breast slices spread out in fan shapes. Serve immediately. *Makes 6 servings.*

Marinade

Combine all ingredients in a large glass bowl.

Papaya Sauce

To prepare sauce, place papaya in a large saucepan over medium-low heat, cover and simmer until fruit begins to liquify, stirring occasionally. Add lemon juice, white wine, salt, pepper and bay leaf, bring to a boil and reduce liquid by half. Remove bay leaf. Transfer sauce mixture to a food processor fitted with the steel blade; puree until smooth. Return sauce to pan, bring back to a simmer and pour in whipping cream. Add cornstarch (mixed with a little water) only if sauce is too thin. Strain through a fine sieve and keep warm.

Red Stripe Chicken

Though any beer you like will work in this recipe, Red Stripe from Jamaica has become the choice of Caribbean lovers in the United States. Its wide distribution makes it a taste of the islands that's both easy to find and affordable.

1 (3-lb.) chicken
1/4 cup vegetable oil
2 cups cream of coconut
About 1 cup Red Stripe beer
1 medium onion, chopped
1 large green bell pepper, chopped
Salt and freshly ground black pepper to taste

Rinse chicken and pat dry. Cut into serving pieces. Heat oil in a Dutch oven over medium heat. Add chicken and brown on all sides. Remove chicken and pour off all oil except 2 tablespoons. Return chicken to pan, then add cream of coconut and beer.

Cover and simmer about 30 minutes or until almost tender. Add onion and bell pepper to chicken. Season to taste with salt and pepper. Simmer about 20 minutes more, until liquid has been reduced to a gravy. If the liquid dries out before chicken is done, add more beer. *Makes 6 servings.*

PICKLED TURKEY

A national dish of Puerto Rico, this preparation belongs to the same family that grew from Spanish pickling including both Mexican *ceviche* and Jamaican escovitched fish. If you skip the initial browning, you can even use this to breathe fresh life into leftover roasted turkey breast.

3 pounds turkey breast, sliced 1/4 inch thick
All-purpose flour
3/4 teaspoon dried leaf oregano
1/2 teaspoon dried leaf basil
1/2 teaspoon dried leaf thyme
Salt and freshly ground black pepper to taste
1/4 cup olive oil
3 medium onions, sliced
1/2 red bell pepper, sliced
1/2 green bell pepper, sliced
1 teaspoon crushed black peppercorns
6 bay leaves
2 garlic cloves, sliced
3/4 cup wine vinegar
20 pimento-stuffed Spanish olives

Dust turkey slices with flour and sprinkle with 1/2 teaspoon oregano, basil and thyme. Season with salt and pepper. Heat 2 tablespoons olive oil in a heavy skillet. Add onions, bell peppers, peppercorns, bay leaves, garlic and remaining 1/4 teaspoon oregano; cook about 25 minutes. Stir in 1/2 cup vinegar and olives.

Heat remaining 2 tablespoons olive oil in another heavy skillet. Add floured turkey slices; cook until golden brown but not overcooked. Place an initial layer of turkey in a deep dish, cover with cooked seasonings and continue in alternating layers. Finish by pouring on any liquid remaining in skillet. Pour remaining 1/4 cup vinegar into skillet and boil 2 minutes to remove turkey drippings. Pour this into dish with turkey. Let cool, then refrigerate. *Makes 6 servings.*

TURKEY & PEPPERS ON SAFFRON RICE

This is a wonderful way to serve turkey. It is more Cuban than anything else, but it has evolved into a Caribbean standard.

Saffron Rice (page 145)
3/4 cup butter or margarine
1-1/2 pounds turkey breast cutlets, pounded very thin
1/2 teaspoon salt
1/4 teaspoon freshly ground black pepper
3 shallots, finely chopped
1 cup dry white wine
3/4 cup Cointreau liqueur
1 red bell pepper, halved, cut into thin strips
1 green bell pepper, halved, cut into thin strips
2 tablespoons vegetable oil
1/2 chicken bouillon cube
1/2 cup whipping cream

Prepare Saffron Rice and transfer it to a 13 x 9-inch baking pan. Add 1/4 of the butter, stirring until it melts in the hot rice. Place in a warm oven.

In a large skillet, melt the remaining 1/2 cup butter. Add turkey cutlets in batches and sauté just until browned. Season with salt and pepper. Place cutlets over the rice and return to warm oven. Add shallots to skillet and cook until tender. Add wine and 1/2 cup of the Cointreau, simmering until reduced by 3/4.

Heat oil in a separate skillet. Add pepper strips; cook until almost tender, then add the remaining Cointreau and set aside. Add bouillon cube and cream to wine-liqueur reduction, cooking over medium heat until slightly thickened. Arrange pepper strips over turkey and rice and pour cream sauce over all. *Makes 6 servings.*

TURKEY STEW

There's hardly anything that walks, swims or flies that an island cook can't turn into a marvelous stew. Turkey has seldom had it so good.

8 pieces turkey, preferably wings and thighs
Salt and freshly ground black pepper to taste
3 tablespoons vegetable oil
1 medium green bell pepper, diced
1 medium onion, finely chopped
1 garlic clove, finely chopped
2 tablespoons all-purpose flour
3-1/2 cups Turkey Stock (page 22), or chicken broth
1-1/4 cups tomato puree
2 tablespoons red wine vinegar
1 Scotch Bonnet or jalapeño chile, finely chopped
3 large potatoes, cut into chunks
1-1/4 cups green peas, thawed if frozen

Cut off and discard the end piece of each wing, then season turkey with salt and pepper. Heat oil in a large pot over medium heat. Add wings and thighs; cook until browned. Set them aside.

Add bell pepper, onion and garlic to mixture of oil and drippings; sauté until just tender. Reduce heat and stir in flour. Blend well. Stir in stock, tomato paste, vinegar and chile. Return turkey pieces to pot and bring to a boil. Reduce heat to low, cover and simmer 2 hours, basting occasionally any turkey pieces not covered with liquid. Remove turkey once again and set it aside. Skim as much fat as possible from liquid in pan, then add potatoes and heat to boiling. Simmer 30 minutes. Meanwhile, debone meat in large chunks. Return meat to pan and add the peas. Cook 10 minutes more to make sure all pieces are heated through. *Makes 6 servings.*

Keshi Yena

An attractive ball of Edam cheese stuffed with chicken, beef or seafood, this has to be one of the most intriguing blends of ethnic groups anywhere.

1 (4-lb.) Edam cheese
2 tablespoons butter or margarine
2 pounds chicken, cooked, deboned, chopped
2 medium onions, chopped
1 large green bell pepper, chopped
3 large tomatoes, chopped
1 tablespoon chopped parsley
1/2 teaspoon salt
1 to 2 Scotch Bonnet or jalapeño chiles, minced
1 cup unseasoned dry bread crumbs
1/4 cup raisins
2 tablespoons pickle relish
1/2 cup chopped pimento-stuffed Spanish olives
2 eggs, beaten

Peel away wax. Cut off the top of the cheese casing and set it aside. Scoop out cheese and reserve, leaving only the 1/2-inch shell. Cover the shell and top with water and soak 1 hour, then drain. Melt butter in a medium saucepan; add chicken, onions, bell pepper, tomatoes, parsley, salt and chile. Cook about 5 minutes.

In a bowl, shred reserved Edam and mix half with bread crumbs, raisins, pickle relish, olives and eggs, reserving remaining cheese for another use. Thoroughly combine chicken mixture with egg mixture. Preheat oven to 350F (175C). Grease a 3-quart casserole dish. Press stuffing into the cheese shell and replace top. Set stuffed shell in greased casserole dish and bake 45 minutes. Let stuffed cheese stand 10 minutes, then peel away and discard outer skin. Cut in wedges and serve hot. *Makes 6 to 8 servings.*

CHICKEN ROTI

Around Trinidad, shops selling roti are as common as fast-food outlets in the United States. Roti is a specific Indian bread stuffed with an endless choice of curries. Here is one of the best. Besides, we love what Trinidadians call this same bread when they rip it up to eat with a dish of curry. They call it Buss-Up-Shut, which translates as "busted-up-shirt"—the torn cloth these pieces resemble.

1/4 cup vegetable oil
1 onion, chopped
4 garlic cloves, minced
1 Scotch Bonnet chile, seeds removed, chopped
1 (2- to 3-lb.) chicken, cut in serving pieces
6 tablespoons Trinidadian curry paste, or Curry Powder (page 27)
4 cups water
Caribbean hot sauce to taste
Roti Bread (see below)
Chutney

ROTI BREAD

3 cups all-purpose flour
3 tablespoons baking powder
1/2 teaspoon salt
1 cup water
Vegetable oil for cooking

Heat the oil in a large skillet over medium heat. Add the onion, garlic and chile and sauté until softened. Add the chicken pieces and the curry paste and cook 3 minutes, stirring occasionally. Add the water and hot sauce, stir and reduce heat to low. Simmer, covered, until chicken is tender, about 30 minutes. Uncover and simmer 15 minutes, to allow the sauce to thicken.

Meanwhile prepare dough for bread. Remove the chicken pieces and cut the meat off the bone. Continue cooking the sauce until thick, then return the chicken meat to the skillet. Stir to heat the mixture through.

Fold the curried chicken in the roti bread and serve warm, accompanied by hot sauce and chutney. *Makes 6 to 8 servings.*

Roti Bread

Sift together the flour, baking powder and salt into a large bowl. Add the water and mix to form a soft dough. Knead on a lightly floured surface and let stand, covered, 30 minutes. Knead again and divide into 4 balls. Roll out on a floured surface as thin as possible, reaching a diameter of 8 to 10 inches.

Heat about 1 tablespoon oil in a large skillet over medium heat. Add one round and cook about 1-1/2 minutes per side. Drizzle additional oil on each side as it cooks. Remove carefully and drain on paper towels. Repeat with remaining rounds and more oil, as needed.   *Makes 4 breads.*

Baked Chicken & Papaya

Chicken and papaya seem as natural a combination in the islands as ham and pineapple do in the States.

3 whole chicken breasts, split
3 tablespoons butter, melted
3/4 cup honey
3/4 cup freshly squeezed lemon or lime juice
6 tablespoons butter or margarine
3/4 teaspoon freshly grated nutmeg
3 papayas, halved, peeled, seeded

Preheat oven to 375F (190C). Line a baking dish with foil. Remove any excess fat from chicken, then brush it with melted butter. Place chicken, meaty side down, in foil-lined pan. Bake in preheated oven 15 minutes.

Meanwhile, prepare a honey glaze by combining honey, lemon juice, butter and nutmeg in a small saucepan. Cook, stirring occasionally, to blend and thicken. Turn chicken and brush with glaze. Cut papaya into 3/4-inch wedges. Cut some wedges in chunks, if desired. Add to chicken. Bake 10 to 15 minutes more, until chicken is done.   *Makes 6 servings.*

SEAFOOD

Older islanders tend to reminisce about the days when seafood was more plentiful in the Caribbean—when the mullet were running, for instance, or when the crab were so thick you could barely walk along the beach. Even in the past, however, seafood tended to be a sometime thing in the region as a whole. After all, the salting of fish to preserve it is a skill as old as the island peoples, one that would have been unnecessary had fresh fish been leaping into every boat.

Even pickled fish shipped from the Old World found a following in the islands, explaining the popularity of dishes like Solomon Gundy. Today, the fact is that one island may be rich in local seafood while another just a few miles across the water is not, a twist of fate based on prevailing currents and coral formations. All islands, though, have rich seafood traditions, most reflecting the ethnic entanglements of their populations.

ESCOVITCHED FISH

Fortunately or unfortunately (depending on your point of view), this dish shares little more than its name and its most basic technique with the Mexican raw fish creation called *ceviche*. The fish here is nicely fried, but the vegetables carry on the ancient Spanish art of pickling.

1 teaspoon freshly ground black pepper
1/2 teaspoon salt
1/4 cup all-purpose flour
2 pounds fish steaks (kingfish, Spanish mackerel or tilefish),
    about 1/2 inch thick
1/2 cup plus 2 tablespoons vegetable oil
1 large Bermuda onion, peeled, cut in half, thinly sliced
2 green bell peppers, sliced in thin rings
2 red bell peppers, sliced in thin rings
1 small Scotch Bonnet or jalapeño chile, thinly sliced
2 tablespoons allspice berries
1/2 cup white wine vinegar

Mix pepper, salt and flour together in a shallow bowl. Dip fish steaks in seasoned flour, shake off any excess and set steaks aside. Heat 1/2 cup of oil in a medium skillet over medium-high heat until very hot but not smoking. Add fish steaks 1 or 2 at a time and fry quickly, about 2 minutes on each side. Drain on paper towels.

When all fish is cooked, arrange steaks in a single layer on a large platter. Wipe skillet clean, reduce heat and add remaining 2 tablespoons oil. Add onion, bell peppers, chile and allspice berries. Cover and cook mixture 5 minutes. Add vinegar and continue cooking 5 minutes more. Pour over fish slices, arranging peppers and onion on top. Serve at room temperature. *Makes 6 servings.*

BRIDGETOWN FLYING FISH

It's a shame the delicate and delicious flying fish, something akin to the mascot of Barbados, isn't more readily available in the United States. Any mild, sweet-tasting fish will work in this recipe. And if you're visiting Barbados, you can now buy flying fish frozen at the airport, carefully packed for the flight home.

1 small onion, minced
1 small green bell pepper, finely chopped
1 tablespoon finely chopped chives
1 teaspoon chopped fresh thyme
1 teaspoon chopped fresh parsley
Salt and freshly ground black pepper to taste
4 or 5 drops freshly squeezed lime juice
8 fillets of flying fish
1 egg, beaten
2 to 3 cups unseasoned dry bread crumbs
Vegetable oil for deep-frying
2 limes, cut into wedges

Mix onion, bell pepper, chives, thyme, parsley, salt, black pepper and lime juice in a small bowl into a paste, then spread this over meaty side of flying fish. Cover and refrigerate 1 hour. Dip each fillet into beaten egg and then into bread crumbs. Heat 2 to 3 inches of oil in a heavy skillet over medium heat. Add fish, in batches; fry about 10 minutes in all, turning once or twice. Serve with lime wedges. *Makes 4 to 6 servings.*

BROILED FISH WITH ORANGE SAUCE

Swordfish works exceptionally well in this presentation, which is highlighted by the sweet and pungent sauce flecked with "confetti" squares.

1/2 cup olive oil
2 garlic cloves, mashed
1 tablespoon chopped fresh parsley
1/2 cup orange juice
Juice of 1 lemon
1 teaspoon freshly ground black pepper
6 lean, firm-fleshed fish steaks, about 1 inch thick
12 pitted ripe olives

ORANGE SAUCE

1/4 cup butter or margarine
1 cup orange juice
1/2 cup white wine
1 small garlic clove, mashed
1/2 teaspoon Dijon-style mustard
1 tablespoon grated orange peel
Peel of 1 orange, cut into thin strips
1 red bell pepper, peeled, cut into tiny squares
6 large pitted ripe olives, cut into tiny squares

Prepare a marinade by mixing oil, garlic, parsley, orange juice, lemon juice and black pepper in a small bowl. Place fish steaks in a single layer in a long pan and rub some of marinade into them, then pour on remaining liquid. Cover and refrigerate 2 hours, turning steaks once. Prepare sauce.

Preheat broiler. Remove fish steaks from marinade and broil them under preheated broiler, about 5 minutes on each side. To serve, place steaks on warmed dinner plates, pour some of sauce over each steak and garnish with 2 ripe olives. *Makes 6 servings.*

ORANGE SAUCE

Melt 3 tablespoons of the butter in a medium saucepan. Add orange juice, wine, garlic, mustard and grated orange peel. Bring to a boil and reduce liquid to about 1/3 its original volume. Pour sauce through a strainer and return it to pan. Bring to a simmer; stir in remaining 1 tablespoon butter. At last minute before serving, add orange peel strips, bell pepper and olive squares to sauce.

SWORDFISH WITH TOMATILLO SAUCE

Tomatillos resemble green tomatoes and are very popular in Puerto Rican cooking. Fresh tomatillos have a thin, paperlike husk that must be removed before using. If fresh tomatillos are not available, canned may be substituted. The beautiful green sauce goes equally well with grilled tuna or shark.

4 swordfish steaks, about 3/4 inch thick
2 tablespoons freshly squeezed lemon juice
8 tomatillos, peeled, chopped
1/4 cup cilantro
1 small Scotch Bonnet or jalapeño chile, seeded, chopped
1/2 cup Fish Stock (page 25), or chicken broth
2 tablespoons butter or margarine
1/4 cup finely chopped onion
Salt and freshly ground black pepper to taste

Preheat grill or broiler. Sprinkle swordfish with lemon juice, cover and set aside. In a blender or food processor fitted with the steel blade, combine tomatillos, cilantro, chile and stock. Process until smooth. Melt butter over medium heat in a medium saucepan. Add onion and cook until golden brown, about 4 minutes. Pour in tomatillo mixture. Simmer until sauce is reduced and thickened, about 5 minutes. Season to taste with salt and black pepper.

Broil or grill swordfish 3 minutes per side, or until still slightly pink in center. Sprinkle with salt and pepper. Serve immediately with tomatillo sauce. *Makes 4 servings.*

SNAPPER SANTIAGO

This whole-fish preparation, named in honor of the village Santiago de Cuba, makes quite an impression when it's carried to the table. It is a classic Cuban recipe.

7 garlic cloves
1/4 teaspoon ground leaf oregano
3 allspice berries
1/2 teaspoon salt
1/2 cup plus 1-1/2 tablespoons orange juice
1/4 cup plus 1-1/2 tablespoons lemon juice
1 (4-lb.) red snapper
3/4 cup coarsely chopped parsley
1 tablespoon dry white wine
3/4 cup olive oil
1/8 teaspoon ground cumin
Salt to taste
2 large baking potatoes, thinly sliced
1 onion, thinly sliced
1 green bell pepper, cut in thin strips
1 red bell pepper, cut in thin strips
1 small jar Spanish-style olives
2 hard-cooked eggs, sliced

Prepare a paste by mashing 4 garlic cloves, oregano, allspice and 1/2 teaspoon salt with a mortar and pestle. Add 1/2 cup orange juice and 1/4 cup lemon juice, mix well and rub into whole snapper inside and out. Cover and refrigerate at least 2 hours. In a food processor fitted with the steel blade, process remaining 3 garlic cloves, 1-1/2 tablespoons orange juice, 1-1/2 tablespoons lemon juice, parsley, white wine, 1/2 cup olive oil, cumin and salt to taste until smooth to make a wine sauce.

Preheat oven to 350F (175C). Grease a baking dish large enough to hold fish. Line it with sliced potatoes. Mix onion with green and red bell peppers, then place this mixture atop potatoes. Season to taste with salt. Set fish on top of vegetables and spoon some wine sauce into its cavity, pouring rest over top. Leave head free of sauce so it will be red when cooked. Bake in preheated oven until fish turns from translucent to opaque, about 1 hour. Remove eyes and replace with olives. Garnish with hard-cooked eggs and remaining olives. *Makes 6 servings.*

RUN DOWN

This is one of the most traditional island dishes, clearly concocted on the spur of some moment from anything and everything close at hand. The name Run Down is Jamaican, but the dish is Caribbean in the broadest possible sense. Run Down is traditionally served with boiled green bananas and simple flour dumplings.

3 tablespoons freshly squeezed lime juice
2 pounds mackerel fillets or other fatty fish
3 cups Coconut Milk (page 26)
1 large onion, finely chopped
2 garlic cloves
1 Scotch Bonnet or jalapeño chile, finely chopped
1 pound tomatoes, peeled, chopped
Salt and freshly ground black pepper to taste
1 teaspoon dried leaf thyme
1 tablespoon vinegar

In a shallow bowl, pour lime juice over fillets and set aside. Cook Coconut Milk in a heavy large skillet until it appears oily, then add onion and garlic, then the chile, tomatoes, salt, pepper, thyme and vinegar. Add fish, cover and cook over medium heat 10 minutes. *Makes 6 servings.*

SPICY GRILLED FISH

Next time you fire up the backyard grill, substitute this wonder for the hamburgers. It's guaranteed to make a fish lover out of just about anybody.

1 teaspoon dried leaf tarragon
1 teaspoon dried leaf basil
1 teaspoon dried leaf thyme
1 teaspoon paprika
1 teaspoon dried leaf oregano
1 teaspoon fennel seeds
1 teaspoon anise seeds
2 tablespoons freshly squeezed lemon juice
2 tablespoons freshly squeezed lime juice
1 tablespoon white wine
2 tablespoons Worcestershire sauce
1 Scotch Bonnet or jalapeño chile, finely chopped
2 cups vegetable oil
6 fillets of mild, light-fleshed fish

Preheat grill. Combine all ingredients except fish in a shallow bowl. Add fish, making sure you cover it well with seasoning paste. Place fish on a hot grill, turning just once when flesh becomes opaque. The charbroiled side should be flecked with brown and lined with a smoky-tasting pattern like a nicely done steak. Remove to dinner plates. *Makes 6 servings.*

FISHERMAN'S STEW

This wonderful stew with memories of the Mediterranean made the trip nicely from the old country to the French West Indies. Its hearty, toss-in-whatever's-handy nature makes it especially appealing to frugal islanders.

1/4 cup vegetable oil
8 small onions, chopped
6 garlic cloves, minced
4 carrots, chopped
4 celery stalks, chopped
8 medium tomatoes, coarsely chopped
2 tablespoons tomato paste
2 teaspoons dried leaf thyme
1 teaspoon dried rosemary
1 teaspoon grated orange peel
2 teaspoons freshly ground black pepper
1 Scotch Bonnet or jalapeño chile, finely chopped
3 (12-oz.) bottles beer
3 cups water
4 (1-lb.) lobsters
1 pound each clams, mussels, oysters, scallops and shrimp
    (or other seafood of your choice)

Heat oil in a large saucepan. Add vegetables; cook until softened. Add tomato paste and seasonings. Cook until onions start to turn transparent, then remove mixture from heat and set it aside. In a separate pot, bring beer and water to a boil. Add lobsters; boil 5 minutes. Add clams, mussels and oysters. Steam 5 more minutes, or until shellfish open. Discard any which do not open. Remove shellfish from liquid. Strain liquid into vegetables, add shrimp and scallops and simmer 4 minutes. Remove lobster from its shell and cut meat into serving pieces. Add it with rest of shellfish to stew. Heat until just heated through. Serve immediately. *Makes 6 servings.*

MINCED LOBSTER

From as far south as the Grenadines to as far north as the Bahamas, Caribbean lobster gets a chance to shine in this peppery favorite. If your supermarket boils or steams lobsters for you (as many are starting to do), you'll find this dish even more of a breeze.

3 (1-lb.) lobsters
1/2 cup vegetable oil
1/3 cup chopped celery
1/2 cup chopped onion
1/2 cup chopped green bell pepper
1/4 cup diced bacon
1/4 cup tomato paste
4 large tomatoes, peeled, seeded, diced
1/2 teaspoon fresh thyme
1/2 teaspoon freshly ground black pepper
1 Scotch Bonnet or jalapeño chile, finely chopped
Salt to taste
1 tablespoon water
Cooked white rice

Bring 6 to 8 inches of water to a boil in a large stockpot. Add lobsters. Partially cover; bring water to a simmer. Cook about 7 minutes. Remove lobsters with tongs. Cool and remove from shell. Shred meat by hand.

Heat oil in a medium skillet over medium-high heat. Add celery, onion, bell pepper, bacon and tomato paste; cook 4 to 5 minutes. Add minced lobster and tomatoes. Cook, stirring often, 4 to 5 minutes more. Add thyme, black pepper, chile, salt to taste and the water. Simmer about 3 minutes to reduce liquid. Serve over rice. *Makes 6 servings.*

Lobster Tails with Tangy Rum Sauce

This dish is wonderfully simple, as some argue lobster should be anyway. Yet it proclaims its island roots in the buttery rum sauce.

6 lobster tails
1/4 cup rum
2 tablespoons butter

Rum Sauce

2 tablespoons lemon juice
1/2 cup butter, melted
1 tablespoon chopped parsley
1/2 teaspoon salt
1 jigger of rum
1/4 teaspoon red (cayenne) pepper
Freshly ground black pepper to taste

Preheat broiler. To prepare lobster tails for broiling, cut away upper shell and crack lower shell to prevent curling under heat. Arrange on a broiling rack unshelled side up. Sprinkle each tail with rum and dot it with butter. Broil 3 inches away from heat 8 minutes. While lobster tails are broiling, prepare sauce. Place 1 lobster tail on each dinner plate and top with sauce. *Makes 6 servings*.

Rum Sauce

Combine all ingredients in a small saucepan. Cook over low heat until hot.

Caribbean Shrimp

The first cooks to serve this dish almost certainly were Chinese immigrants to the Caribbean, who brought their skills for quick-frying from the old country. Now, however, the dish is "generic Caribbean." If you order Caribbean Shrimp in the United States, this is what you'll probably get. I only hope it tastes this good.

24 medium shrimp, about 1 pound
1 egg
1 cup all-purpose flour
1/2 cup beer, preferably Red Stripe
1/2 tablespoon baking powder
1 tablespoon salt
1/2 tablespoon freshly ground black pepper
1/2 tablespoon red (cayenne) pepper
1/2 tablespoon paprika
1 tablespoon garlic powder
1/2 teaspoon dried leaf thyme
1/2 teaspoon dried leaf oregano
1-1/2 cups grated coconut
Vegetable oil for frying
1 cup orange marmalade
1/4 cup Dijon-style mustard
1/8 teaspoon ground ginger

Peel and devein shrimp, leaving tails on. In a bowl, combine egg with 3/4 cup of the flour, the beer and baking powder. In another bowl, mix remaining flour with herbs and spices. Holding tail, dip each shrimp first in batter, then in seasoned flour and shake off excess. Sprinkle each shrimp liberally with grated coconut and set aside on a baking sheet.

Heat oil in a deep skillet over medium heat. Add shrimp 1 at a time. Cook until golden brown on all sides, turning once. Drain on paper towels. Prepare a sauce by mixing marmalade, mustard and ginger in a small bowl. Spoon sauce into 6 small bowls. Place bowls on 6 appetizer plates. Surround bowls with 4 shrimp per serving. *Makes 6 servings.*

BAKED SHRIMP IN BANANA LEAVES

Though this recipe works just about as well with foil or parchment paper, the banana leaves add a touch of seaside cooking in the tropics.

1 pound uncooked medium shrimp
2 onions, finely chopped
2 garlic cloves, finely chopped
1-1/2 cups shredded coconut
Salt to taste
4 teaspoons freshly squeezed lime juice
3 tomatoes, thinly sliced

Peel shrimp and set aside in a medium bowl. Puree onions and garlic in a blender, then pour this puree over shrimp. In another bowl, blend coconut with salt to taste and lime juice. Add this to shrimp, mix well, cover and marinate at least 1 hour.

Preheat oven to 350F (175C). Line a casserole dish with banana leaves. Place a layer of tomatoes on banana leaves, then spread with shrimp mixture. Top with remaining tomatoes and an additional layer of banana leaves. (If parchment paper is used, fold it over top and seal by pressing with fingers.) Bake in preheated oven 40 minutes. Serve hot.   *Makes 6 servings.*

La Barquilla de Piña

This presentation, which hails from the north coast of Puerto Rico, has to be one of the most attractive ways of serving seafood anywhere. Chunks of lobster tail (or whole tails of small lobsters) work equally well.

6 medium pineapples
3 tablespoons butter
4 pounds large shrimp, peeled, deveined
1 pound fresh mushrooms, sliced
1 cup rum
1/4 cup sherry
1 quart whipping cream
1 teaspoon freshly squeezed lemon juice
1 recipe Hollandaise Sauce (page 20)

Peel and halve pineapples. Discard tops. Scoop out fruit to form a "boat," reserving fruit for another use.

Melt butter in a large skillet over medium-high heat. Add shrimp and mushrooms. Cook only until shrimp turn pink. Pour in rum and sherry. Ignite, either by tilting pan over a gas flame or lighting carefully with a long-stemmed match. When flames have burned out, pour in cream and boil until thickened. Add lemon juice.

Preheat broiler. Divide shrimp-mushroom mixture among pineapple boats and top each with Hollandaise Sauce. Set boats under broiler until sauce is lightly browned. *Makes 12 servings.*

GRILLED SHRIMP WITH TAMARIND BUTTER

Long before grilling became trendy, islanders were cooking outdoors and thinking it was old-fashioned—which of course it is. You'll be delighted by the marriage of these marinated and grilled shrimp with the spicy dipping sauce.

2 pounds uncooked medium shrimp
1 cup freshly squeezed orange juice
1 cup coconut oil
1 pound butter, softened
1/4 cup tamarind paste (available at Oriental groceries)
1/4 cup unsweetened dried coconut, chopped, toasted
Salt and freshly ground black pepper
Coconut extract to taste

Prepare shrimp for marinating by removing their legs and underside of tail shell. Whisk together orange juice and coconut oil in a large bowl. Add shrimp, then cover and refrigerate overnight.

Whip butter with a wire whisk until it is light and fluffy. Dissolve tamarind paste in 2 tablespoons of boiling water and add it to butter. Stir in coconut, salt, pepper and coconut extract to taste, starting with 1/2 teaspoon of extract. Refrigerate overnight, removing to soften approximately 3 hours before serving. The tamarind butter should be soft but not runny.

Preheat charcoal grill. Drain shrimp. Skewer shrimp on small skewers. Grill until shrimp are just pink. Serve hot skewers of shrimp with individual bowls of tamarind butter for dipping. *Makes 6 servings*.

Shrimp with Roasted Garlic & Papaya

This recipe makes use of that wonderfully unexpected combination of papaya and lots of garlic, which quickly sets these sautéed shrimp apart from the wide array of others.

18 large shrimp
2 garlic heads, peeled
1/2 cup butter or margarine
1 celery stalk, finely chopped
1 medium onion, finely chopped
2-1/4 cups dry white wine
1 bay leaf
1 quart Fish Stock (page 25), or chicken broth
1 pint (2 cups) whipping cream
2 papayas
Chopped fresh thyme and basil to taste
Salt and freshly ground black pepper to taste

Preheat oven to 350F (175C). Peel and devein shrimp, then set them aside. Add garlic and 1/4 cup butter to a baking pan; cook until lightly browned, 10 minutes. Melt 2 tablespoons butter in a medium saucepan. Add browned garlic, celery and onion; cook until onion is transparent. Add 2 cups wine, bay leaf and stock. Reduce liquid by half over high heat, then stir in cream.

Cut papayas in half, remove seeds and peel. Slice papayas into long thin strips and toss these in a medium bowl with basil and thyme; set aside. Melt remaining 2 tablespoons butter in a large skillet. Add shrimp; cook until pink, about 4 minutes, adding 1/4 cup wine during last 2 minutes of cooking. Season to taste with salt and pepper. Spoon sauce onto 6 warmed dinner plates, set strips of papaya in center of each and surround with 3 cooked shrimp per serving. *Makes 6 servings.*

SHRIMP-STUFFED PEPPERS

The banana provides an unexpected accent to the shrimp in this stuffed pepper from Barbados.

8 medium green bell peppers
1 cup cooked, peeled small shrimp
1-1/2 cups cooked rice
3 medium tomatoes, chopped
1 medium onion, chopped
1 garlic clove, crushed
1 tablespoon chopped parsley
1 tablespoon chopped fresh thyme
1 banana, finely chopped
4 or 5 drops of freshly squeezed lime juice
1/4 cup Chicken Stock (page 23)

Preheat oven to 375F (190C). Cut stem end off each pepper; cut off stems. Remove seeds and rinse peppers, then trim a little from bottoms so they will stand upright. Set them side by side in a baking dish.

Mix together all remaining ingredients except stock and stuff this mixture into peppers. Place tops back on peppers. Pour stock around stuffed peppers. Bake in preheated oven 30 to 40 minutes, until peppers are tender. *Makes 4 servings, 2 peppers each.*

CRAB BACKS

These are known in some parts of the United States as Stuffed Crab. Leave it to the islands to give them a name with a down-home, soulfood spin.

12 live blue crabs
3 tablespoons butter
1 medium onion, chopped
1 medium tomato, chopped
3 tablespoons chopped chives
1 tablespoon Worcestershire sauce
Salt and freshly ground black pepper to taste
Unseasoned dry bread crumbs

Bring water to boil in a large pot. Add live crabs, pushing them down with a wooden spoon. Boil 15 minutes, until shells turn a bright red. Drain and cool. Break open claws and pick out meat. Discard pieces of shell from claws. Carefully open crab backs, removing and reserving any meat and fat but discarding gill and white intestine. Scrub empty shells thoroughly.

Preheat broiler. Melt butter in a medium saucepan over medium-high heat. Add onion, tomato and chives; cook until softened. Remove from heat. Stir in flaked crabmeat, Worcestershire sauce, salt and black pepper. Refill crab backs with crab mixture; sprinkle with bread crumbs. Place stuffed crab on a baking sheet; brown under preheated broiler. Serve hot. *Makes 6 servings*.

CRABMEAT ST. BARTS

During the season on St. Barthelemy, not only do jet-setters never call the island by its full name but they bask in the wonders of classic French cuisine. This traditional gratin is energized by the addition of Caribbean chiles and rum.

1 cup milk
2 or 3 Scotch Bonnet or jalapeño chiles, minced
1 bouquet garni (thyme, bay leaf and parsley tied together)
Salt and freshly ground black pepper to taste
2 cups unseasoned dry bread crumbs
1 pound crabmeat
1/4 pound bacon, cut into 1/4-inch pieces
3 tablespoons minced onion
3 tablespoons finely chopped fresh chives
3 tablespoons minced fresh parsley
1 teaspoon minced fresh thyme
1/4 cup butter or margarine
2 tablespoons freshly squeezed lime juice
Dark rum to taste

In a heavy saucepan, combine milk, half of the chiles, the bouquet garni, salt and pepper; bring to a boil. Reduce heat and simmer 15 minutes, then cool completely and strain into a bowl. Add bread crumbs and let them soak up liquid 15 minutes. Then squeeze out any excess liquid and mix bread crumbs in a bowl with crabmeat. In a small skillet, fry bacon with remaining chiles until crisp. Remove using a slotted spoon and drain on paper towels. Stir bacon, onion and herbs into crabmeat mixture.

Melt butter in a medium skillet over medium-high heat. Add crab mixture; cook, stirring, about 10 minutes, until browned. Blend in lime juice and rum to taste. Preheat oven to 300F (150C). Butter 10 small baking dishes and divide crab mixture among them. Arrange on baking sheets. Bake in preheated oven until heated through, about 10 minutes. *Makes 10 servings.*

GROUPER ST. MARTIN

The French side of St. Martin (an island with a Dutch side too!) gives us this recipe for grouper with a bright Creole sauce featuring eggplant.

4 tablespoons vegetable oil
1 cup diced eggplant
1/2 cup diced green bell pepper
1/2 cup diced onion
1 tomato, diced
1 garlic clove, minced
1 cup canned crushed tomatoes
1/4 cup water
1/2 cup cooked okra, chopped
1 teaspoon dried oregano
1/2 teaspoon Caribbean hot pepper sauce
Ground black, white and red pepper to taste
Salt to taste
4 grouper fillets
1/2 cup all-purpose flour
1 lime, quartered

In a saucepan, heat 2 tablespoons of the oil over medium heat. Add the eggplant, bell pepper, onion, fresh tomato and garlic and sauté until softened, stirring occasionally. Add the crushed tomatoes, water, okra and seasonings. Bring to a simmer. Cook 5 minutes over low heat, stirring.

Heat the remaining oil in a skillet over medium heat. Dredge the grouper lightly in the flour. Add to the skillet and cook 5 to 7 minutes per side or until grouper just begins to flake. Remove the fillets to warm serving plates and spoon the eggplant sauce on top. Serve garnished with lime wedges. *Makes 4 servings.*

BROWN STEW FISH

Jamaicans love gravy and just about anything that can be served with it. Here is a very simple, old-fashioned recipe that islanders relish—even those who cook fancy dishes in hotels and restaurants.

1 tablespoon vegetable oil
6 fish fillets
All-purpose flour
2 medium onions, chopped
2 tomatoes, chopped
2 green onions, chopped
3 carrots, chopped
1/2 pound green beans, chopped in thirds
1 quart fish stock or water

Heat the oil in a large skillet over medium heat. Dredge the fish lightly in the flour. Add to the skillet and cook until golden brown, turning once. Remove the fish and set aside. Strain most of the oil from the skillet, then add all the vegetables and cook until crisp-tender, stirring occasionally. Pour in the stock or water and simmer until the flavors blend, about 10 minutes.

Return the fish to the sauce, cover and simmer until heated through. *Makes 6 servings.*

STEAMED FISH & FISH TEA

Here are two traditional dishes re-created as one by chef Everett Wilkerson of the San Souci resort in Ocho Rios. It's a lengthy process, but a surprisingly simple one as well. The result is lovely.

8 (8-oz.) whole fish such as tilapia, ready to cook
Water
3 carrots, diced
1 large onion, minced
12 okra pods, sliced
2 chayotes, diced
2 medium potatoes, peeled and diced
1 small pumpkin, cleaned and diced
2 sprigs fresh thyme
1 to 2 Scotch Bonnet chiles, minced
2 green onions, minced
1 teaspoon minced garlic
Salt and fresh ground black pepper to taste
3 cups water

FISH SEASONING

1 green onion, minced
1 sprig fresh thyme
1 teaspoon minced garlic
1 medium tomato, diced
1 Scotch Bonnet chile, minced
1/4 cup lime juice
Salt and freshly ground black pepper to taste

Fillet the fish and place the bones in a pot with cold water to cover. Bring to a boil, then simmer 10 minutes. Skim any froth from the top, then add about 1/3 of the carrot and onion. Simmer 20 to 25 minutes more. Strain and discard the bones and vegetables.

Prepare Fish Seasoning and use to season the fish fillets. Using a steamer, steam the fillets over the stock 10 minutes or until fish turns from translucent to opaque and reserve, covered, in a warm place. Add the remaining ingredients to the stock and simmer 10 minutes. Season to taste with salt and pepper.

Serve the fish tea either under or over the steamed fish fillets. *Makes 8 servings.*

FISH SEASONING

Combine all ingredients in a small bowl.

SHARK & BAKE

Fish and chips never had it so good as this roadside variant from Trinidad and Tobago. Shark is fairly easy to get anywhere these days, but catfish is a reasonable substitute.

1 lime
1 pound shark fillets, cut in pieces 4 inches long and 1 inch wide
2 garlic cloves, minced
2 green onions, finely chopped
1 teaspoon minced fresh thyme
1 teaspoon salt
2 cups all-purpose flour, seasoned with salt and pepper
Vegetable oil for frying
Bakes (page 167)
Caribbean hot pepper sauce

Squeeze the lime juice over the shark and let stand 5 minutes. Combine the garlic, green onions, thyme and salt in a shallow bowl. Dip the shark into the garlic mixture, then into the seasoned flour.

Cover the bottom of a large skillet with oil and heat over medium heat. Add the shark, a few pieces at a time, and cook until golden brown, turning once. Drain the fish on paper towels and serve wrapped in bakes. Sprinkle with hot sauce to taste. *Makes 2 to 4 servings.*

BLAFF

To Caribbean ears, "blaff" is the sound a fish makes when it's slipped into this poaching liquid. Try the recipe at home—perhaps you'll hear it too!

5 cups water
3/4 cup lime juice
1-1/2 pounds fresh fish (snapper, marlin, swordfish)
1 medium onion, diced
2 cloves garlic, minced
1 Scotch Bonnet chile
1 tablespoon minced fresh parsley
1 tablespoon fresh thyme
10 to 12 allspice berries
1 teaspoon salt

In a shallow baking dish, combine 1 cup of the water with 1/2 cup of the lime juice, add fish and marinate in the refrigerator 2 hours, turning after 1 hour. Drain and discard the marinade.

Pour the remaining water into a saucepan, along with the remaining lime juice and all remaining ingredients except fish. Bring to a rolling boil and boil 3 to 4 minutes, then add the fish and simmer 8 to 10 minutes or until fish flakes easily with a fork.

Remove the fish with a slotted spatula and transfer to warm plates. Spoon the broth over the fish and serve immediately.   *Makes 4 servings.*

LOBSTER SAN SOUCI

This recipe takes several traditional Jamaican lobster dishes and presses them into world-class service. Served just feet away from the lapping Caribbean, the chef's preferred presentation is a sight to behold.

1 large carrot, chopped
1 medium onion, chopped
1 bay leaf
10 whole black peppercorns
4 cups water
1-1/2 cups clarified butter
1/2 teaspoon annatto seeds
1/2 teaspoon fresh thyme leaves
2 teaspoons finely chopped lemon grass
1/2 teaspoon minced garlic
1 green onion, minced
1 eggplant, thinly sliced into rounds
Salt and freshly ground black pepper to taste
8 Caribbean rock lobster tails
1 cup cooked kernel corn
1 Scotch Bonnet chile, minced
1/4 cup grated coconut
1 cup whipping cream

Place the carrot, onion, bay leaf, peppercorns and the water in a large pot. Simmer until the carrot is soft, about 10 minutes. Strain and reserve the liquid as stock.

In a shallow pan over medium heat, combine the clarified butter, annatto, thyme, lemon grass, garlic and green onion. Heat until hot.

Coat the eggplant with butter mixture and fry in a preheated skillet. Season to taste with salt and pepper. Reserve in a warm place.

Using the stock, simmer the lobster tails 12 to 13 minutes or until the meat turns from translucent to opaque. Remove from the stock and let rest. Quickly sauté the corn and the chile with a little of the butter mixture in a skillet. Cover with the grated coconut and the cream. Cook 4 to 5 minutes, until the liquid has become quite thick. Salt and pepper to taste.

Serve the lobster tails with the eggplant rounds and coconut-corn sauce, with the remaining butter mixture on the side. *Makes 8 servings.*

YUCATAN STUFFED CHILES

Around the Mexican Caribbean, these *chiles rellenos de mariscos* are one of the most intriguing items—particularly in thatch-roofed restaurants right on the water.

1 tablespoon butter
1 medium onion, minced
2 garlic cloves, minced
2 fresh Scotch Bonnet chiles, stems and seeds removed
1 pound cooked mixed shellfish, diced
3 tablespoons chopped fresh cilantro
1 teaspoon dried oregano
4 tablespoons salsa, homemade or commercial, plus extra for serving
4 fresh poblano chiles, roasted and peeled
All-purpose flour for dredging
3 eggs, separated
1 tablespoon water
3 tablespoons all-purpose flour
1/4 teaspoon salt
Vegetable oil for frying
Salsa

Melt the butter in a saucepan over medium heat. Add the onion, garlic and Scotch Bonnet chiles and sauté until softened. Add the seafood, cilantro, oregano and salsa. Slit the side of each poblano and fill with the seafood mixture. Dredge the poblanos in the flour.

Beat the egg whites until stiff peaks form. In another bowl, beat the egg yolks with the water, flour and salt until creamy. Fold the yolks into the whites. Dip the stuffed chiles in this mixture until they are coated.

Heat 2 to 3 inches of oil in a large skillet over medium heat. Add stuffed chiles and fry 2 to 3 minutes, until golden brown. Drain on paper towels. Serve with additional salsa. *Makes 4 servings.*

SHRIMP & CRAB PILAU

Trinidad is best known for the paellalike rice dish known as *pilau,* though other islands with traditions of East Indian immigration have the wonder as well. This rendition showcases both shrimp and crabmeat.

1/4 cup butter
1 medium onion, minced
3 cloves garlic, minced
1 Scotch Bonnet chile, minced
1 tomato, diced
2 tablespoons Curry Powder (page 27)
Salt and freshly ground black pepper to taste
1-1/2 cups uncooked white rice
3 cups unsweetened coconut milk
1/2 pound crabmeat, picked over
20 large shrimp, peeled and deveined
1 cup cooked pigeon peas

Melt the butter in a saucepan over medium heat. Add the vegetables and sauté 5 to 7 minutes or until softened, stirring occasionally. Add the seasonings and sauté 2 minutes. Stir in the rice and cook 2 more minutes, coating the rice with the seasoning mix. Add the coconut milk and cook over low heat 20 minutes.

Gently add the crabmeat, shrimp and pigeon peas, reduce heat and cook until the rice has absorbed all the liquid and the shrimp are firm and pink, 5 to 10 minutes. Serve with warm bread. *Makes 4 servings.*

MEATS

The serving of beef in the Caribbean was traditionally (and sometimes still is) a barometer of a family's financial health. British-style roasts and American-style steaks mark the top of the monetary heap; the more austere the circumstances, the cheaper the cut and the more secondary its role to other, cheaper ingredients. Fortunately for lovers of Caribbean food, what a good cook can do with a little beef, a potful of vegetables and a generous handful of spices is miraculous.

Pork is another story, since wild pigs were part of the island scene long before the Spaniards taught the Indians about domestication. Many of the islands' best-loved recipes revolve around pork—starting with the mouth-singeing Jerk Pork and working its way up and down the sophistication scale. Young goat is a Caribbean tradition as well, and even long-unavailable lamb is starting to fire the island imagination.

BEEF-STUFFED PLANTAINS

Though most of the plantains sold on Barbados come from other islands nearby, the Bajans have come up with one of the most creative recipes for using them.

6 bacon slices
3 large ripe plantains
3/4 pound ground beef
2 medium onions, chopped
2 garlic cloves, crushed
1 green bell pepper, chopped
2 medium tomatoes, chopped
1/2 teaspoon dried leaf oregano
Salt and freshly ground black pepper to taste
2 eggs, beaten
Vegetable oil for deep-frying

In a large saucepan, fry bacon until crisp; set slices aside. Slice each plantain lengthwise into 4 strips. Sauté sliced plantains in the bacon fat until they are golden, then drain on paper towels. Cool, then shape each plantain slice into a circle and secure with a wooden pick.

To make filling, brown ground beef in remaining bacon fat, then add onions, garlic, bell pepper, tomatoes, oregano, salt and pepper. Crumble bacon and add to filling. Cook, stirring occasionally, until onions and bell pepper are tender, about 20 minutes.

Fill each plantain circle with filling. Heat 3 inches of oil in a deep heavy pan to 375F (190C) or until a 1-inch bread cube turns golden brown in 50 seconds. Dip filled plantain circles into beaten eggs. Deep-fry in hot oil until golden brown, turning once.   *Makes 4 to 6 servings.*

BEEF & OKRA

Beef gets an unusual African treatment in this dish, which pairs it with tomatoes and okra.

3 pounds beef round steak
Salt and freshly ground black pepper to taste
1/2 cup vegetable oil
3 onions, chopped
2 garlic cloves, chopped
1 thyme sprig
3 tomatoes, chopped
5 cups water
1 pound okra, trimmed

Thinly slice meat, cutting across the grain. Season with salt and pepper. Heat oil in a large pot. Add beef slices in batches; cook until browned. Add onions and garlic. Cook, stirring, until onions just begin to brown. Stir in thyme, tomatoes and the water. Bring mixture to a boil, then reduce heat, cover and simmer 1 to 1-1/2 hours, until meat is tender. Add more water if necessary. When meat is tender, add okra, cover and cook 30 minutes more. Serve hot in bowls. *Makes 6 servings.*

GRILLED VEAL ROULADES WITH FINGER BANANAS & TAMARIND SAUCE

The tamarind sauce is very tart, but it makes a pleasing contrast to the grilled veal and bananas. Miniature finger bananas are especially sweet and tasty, but larger bananas can be substituted. Tamarind nectar and pulp can be found in Spanish and Indian markets.

2 cups tamarind nectar
1/4 cup dried tamarind pulp
2 cups beef broth
1/4 cup rum
8 finger bananas, or 2 medium bananas
1 pound veal cutlets, flattened, cut into 16 pieces

In a medium saucepan, combine tamarind nectar and pulp over medium heat. Bring to a simmer; cook, stirring occasionally, 20 minutes. Add broth and rum; cook 25 minutes. Strain sauce, discarding pulp. If sauce is too thin, return it to pan and simmer until it is reduced to 1-1/2 cups.

Preheat grill or broiler. Cut finger bananas in half lengthwise, or cut medium bananas in half crosswise and then into quarters lengthwise. Wrap a piece of veal cutlet around each piece of banana to make roulades. Thread roulades onto 4 metal skewers. Grill or broil 4 inches from heat 4 minutes on each side, until veal is lightly browned. Serve immediately with tamarind sauce on the side. *Makes 4 servings.*

ROAST VEAL WITH BLACK SAUCE

This delicious veal roast of Puerto Rican inspiration is, with its sauce of beer and brown sugar, truly a superb blending of bitter and sweet.

4 black peppercorns, cracked
1/2 teaspoon ground cloves
1-1/2 teaspoons dried leaf oregano
4 teaspoons salt
1 tablespoon olive oil
1 tablespoon cider vinegar
1-1/2 cups gold rum
1 (4-lb.) veal roast, butterflied
1/4 cup diced ham
6 prunes, pitted, halved
12 pimento-stuffed Spanish olives
1-1/2 cups packed brown sugar
3 cups beer

Make a marinade by mixing together peppercorns, cloves, oregano, salt, olive oil, vinegar and rum in a large glass bowl. Add roast and marinate overnight.

Next day combine ham, prunes and olives in a small bowl; set aside. Drain meat, reserving marinade. Cut several slits in roast and stuff with ham mixture. Roll roast and tie with string. Place in a roasting pan. Add sugar and beer to reserved marinade; pour over roast.

Preheat oven to 350F (175C). Roast in preheated oven about 2 hours until internal temperature of meat reaches 165F (75C). Baste frequently. Let roast stand 15 to 20 minutes before slicing. Pour off sauce, degrease and reduce until syrupy in a saucepan over high heat. Serve alongside the roast. *Makes 8 servings.*

Rum-Glazed Ribs with Tropical Fruit

This dish, with its glistening glazed ribs and skewers of tropical fruit, strikes me as a carnival of Caribbean colors and tastes.

5 pounds pork spareribs
Meat Marinade, see below
Fruit Marinade, see below
4 to 5 cups tropical fruit, cut in bite-size pieces

Meat Marinade

1/2 cup soy sauce
1/4 cup vinegar
2 tablespoons honey or molasses
1 cup Beef Stock (page 24)
1 teaspoon dry mustard
1 garlic clove, minced
1/2 cup rum

Fruit Marinade

1/2 cup orange juice
1/2 cup rum
1 tablespoon sugar
1/8 teaspoon ground ginger

Cut apart spareribs and parboil in water to cover about 1 hour. Prepare Meat Marinade. Remove spareribs from the water, drain and add them to bowl of marinade, turning to coat on all sides. Cover and refrigerate 4 hours or overnight.

Prepare Fruit Marinade. Add fruit; marinate 2 hours. When the ribs and fruit have marinated, preheat oven to 350F (175C). Arrange ribs in a baking pan. Bake ribs about 30 minutes, turning and basting often with their marinade until glazed and golden brown.

While ribs are baking, arrange the fruit with alternating colors and shapes on 6 short skewers. The fruit can be served cold or placed under broiler until sizzling hot. Arrange sparerib and fruit kabobs in a serving dish. *Makes 6 servings.*

MEAT MARINADE

Combine all ingredients in a large glass bowl or plastic bag.

FRUIT MARINADE

Combine all ingredients in a large glass bowl or plastic bag.

TRIPE & BEANS

Needless to say, tripe is not everyone's favorite dish, yet it does have its admirers in the Caribbean as well as in Europe. Tripe, the lining of the cow's stomach, varies a great deal in texture. Honeycomb tripe is considered the finest.

3 pounds tripe, rinsed, cut in small pieces
3 onions, chopped
3 green onions, chopped
2 garlic cloves, chopped
1 thyme sprig
3 tablespoons Curry Powder (page 27), or favorite commercial curry
    powder
2 tomatoes, chopped
1 Scotch Bonnet or jalapeño chile, chopped
Salt and freshly ground black pepper to taste
1 pound lima beans, cooked

Place tripe in a large saucepan with enough water to cover. Bring to a boil, then reduce heat and simmer until tender, about 2 hours. Add onions, green onions, garlic, thyme, Curry Powder, tomatoes and chile. Season to taste with salt and pepper. Simmer 5 minutes, then add the beans. Cook 5 to 10 minutes more, until the liquid is a thick gravy. *Makes 6 servings.*

JERK PORK

To my way of thinking, Jerk Pork is one of the Caribbean's greatest contributions to world cuisine. Developed by the Arawaks and raised to a high art by runaway Jamaican slaves called Maroons, the technique combines a great way of preserving meat in the wild with one of the spiciest, smokiest, most exciting taste combinations you'll find anywhere on earth. Island cooks guard their jerk recipes religiously, but this formula captures the flavors of the very best. True jerk lovers, by the way, travel to the smoky tin sheds on Jamaica's remote Boston Bay the way other pilgrims head for Jerusalem or Mecca.

1/3 cup allspice berries
7 green onions, chopped
3 Scotch Bonnet or jalapeño chiles, chopped
2 garlic cloves
4 thyme sprigs
5 fresh cinnamon leaves or bay leaves
Salt and freshly ground black pepper to taste
5 pounds thick-cut pork loin chops, or any other pork cut

To prepare spice paste, heat allspice berries in a small skillet. Stir 5 minutes, then place berries in a mortar and pound them until they are powdery. Add onions, chiles, garlic, thyme, cinnamon leaves, salt and pepper; grind this mixture together until you have a paste.

Rinse and pat dry pork, then cover it with the peppery paste. Cover and marinate at least 1 hour, or preferably overnight in the refrigerator.

Preheat grill. Place the seasoned meat on medium-hot grill and cook about 1 hour, turning the pork once. If desired, toss some allspice leaves, allspice berries or bay leaves onto the coals for more flavor. Jerk Pork can be served in whole chops, or it can be deboned, chopped up and placed on a strip of banana leaf with a sliced raw onion. *Makes 6 servings.*

CUBAN PORK ROAST

This flavorful pork preparation from Cuba is, in some ways, the ancient Indians' Jerk Pork after the Spanish added their special touches. The tomatoes are a new touch, as is the notion of a sauce to spoon over the meat.

1 (3-lb.) pork loin or shoulder roast, boned, rolled, tied
3 garlic cloves, slivered
4 Scotch Bonnet or jalapeño chiles, chopped
1 medium green bell pepper, coarsely chopped
1 onion, coarsely chopped
2 garlic cloves, minced
1 teaspoon ground cumin
1 teaspoon dried leaf basil
1 teaspoon freshly ground black pepper
1/2 teaspoon ground cinnamon
1 bay leaf
Juice of 2 limes
1 (15-ounce) can tomato puree

Using the tip of a small knife, make slits on top and bottom of roast. Stuff garlic slivers into the slits and set roast in a large bowl. To prepare a marinade, place a large skillet over medium-high heat; add chiles, bell pepper, onion, garlic, cumin, basil, pepper, cinnamon and bay leaf. Cook, stirring, until vegetables are lightly charred, remove skillet from heat and stir in lime juice. Pour over the roast and turn to coat thoroughly. Cover with plastic wrap and refrigerate overnight, turning occasionally.

Preheat oven to 350F (175C). Remove roast from marinade and place in a roasting pan, reserving marinade. Cook the roast 35 minutes per pound, or until a meat thermometer registers 165F (75C).

Combine the tomato puree with the reserved marinade in a small saucepan. Bring to a boil, then reduce heat and simmer 5 minutes. Taste and adjust seasonings. Remove bay leaf. Strain, if desired. Transfer the roast to a serving platter and let stand 10 minutes before slicing. Spoon the sauce over the sliced meat. *Makes 6 servings.*

Skewered Pork & Bay Leaves

Most cooks use bay leaves in stews, soups and other slow-cooked dishes with liquid. This preparation uses them both in the marinade and threaded onto the skewers.

2 pounds lean pork shoulder, cut into 1-inch cubes
18 whole bay leaves
1/2 cup vegetable oil
1/3 cup red wine vinegar
1 small onion, minced
2 Scotch Bonnet or jalapeño chiles, chopped
2 teaspoons salt
1/4 teaspoon freshly ground black pepper
1/4 teaspoon garlic powder
2 green bell peppers, cut into 1-inch squares
12 cherry tomatoes

Place pork and bay leaves in a bowl just large enough to hold them. Combine oil, vinegar, onion, chiles, salt, black pepper and garlic powder in a separate bowl, then pour over meat and mix to coat. Cover and marinate in refrigerator at least 2 hours, stirring occasionally.

Preheat grill. Drain the pork and bay leaves, reserving marinade. On 6 skewers, alternately thread pork, bay leaves and bell peppers. Brush with the reserved marinade. Place on a rack over hot coals and grill until the pork is cooked through, 15 to 20 minutes. Brush frequently with the marinade. About 5 minutes before the end of cooking time, place 2 cherry tomatoes at the end of each skewer and return to the grill until hot. *Makes 6 servings.*

PORK & BANANA STEW

Here's an intriguing stew in which the banana does double duty. The bananas should be firm enough to fill in for a starch such as potato, yet they should be ripe enough to contribute sweetness.

1/2 cup all-purpose flour
Salt and freshly ground black pepper to taste
2 pounds boneless pork, cubed
2 tablespoons vegetable oil
2 medium onions, sliced
1 celery stalk, chopped
1 green bell pepper, chopped
1 red bell pepper, chopped
1 garlic clove, minced
1 Scotch Bonnet or jalapeño chile, finely chopped
2 cups water
1 medium cucumber, peeled, seeded, diced
4 medium tomatoes, chopped
4 firm but ripe bananas, sliced
Cooked white rice

Combine flour, salt and black pepper in a medium bowl. Dredge pork cubes in flour mixture. Shake off excess flour. Heat oil in a large saucepan. Add floured pork; cook, in batches, until browned. Remove pork from the pan.

Add onions, celery, bell peppers, garlic and chile; cook 10 minutes. Return pork to pan and add the water. Bring to a boil, then reduce heat and simmer until the pork is tender, 45 to 60 minutes. Add the cucumber and tomatoes; cook 10 minutes. Add bananas; heat only until they are hot. Serve with rice. *Makes 6 servings*.

MRS. MULLINGS' BAKED PORK CHOPS

Mrs. Mullings (nobody seems to call this wonderful woman by a first name) used to be Erroll Flynn's private cook when he hung out in Port Antonio, Jamaica. Though she says his favorite breakfast was raw dolphin on the dock and his favorite lunch was virtually any alcoholic liquid, she occasionally sneaked in her amazing pork chops. They are now served at her Port Antonio inn, DeMontevin Lodge.

6 thick-cut pork chops
Salt and freshly ground black pepper to taste
1 garlic clove, minced
2 tablespoons vegetable oil
1 Scotch Bonnet or jalapeño chile, minced
2 medium onions
1 large tomato
1 green bell pepper
1/4 cup butter
1/2 cup water
1 thyme sprig
Guava jelly or applesauce

Preheat oven to 350F (175C). Rinse and dry pork chops, then season with salt and pepper. Sprinkle with garlic. Heat oil in a large skillet over medium heat. Add pork chops; brown on both sides.

Transfer the pork chops to a baking pan. Coarsely chop chile, onions, tomato and bell pepper and spread over chops. Add butter, water and thyme. Cover and bake until tender but not dry, about 35 minutes. Serve with guava jelly or applesauce. *Makes 6 servings.*

SPARERIBS CARIBE

If you want to be an authentic island cook, you've got to cure yourself of reaching for the bottle of barbecue sauce every time you fire up the coals. This delicious Caribbean sauce is incredibly easy to make.

3 pounds meaty pork ribs, cut into individual ribs
1/4 cup packed brown sugar
1/4 cup dry sherry
2 tablespoons vinegar
2 tablespoons Worcestershire sauce
1 teaspoon salt
1/2 teaspoon ground ginger
1 (14-oz.) can crushed pineapple
1 teaspoon hot pepper sauce
1/4 cup shredded coconut

Blanch ribs in simmering salted water 30 minutes; drain. Preheat broiler. In a medium saucepan, combine the brown sugar, sherry, vinegar, Worcestershire sauce, salt and ginger. Bring to a boil, add the crushed pineapple with juice and simmer 5 minutes. Remove from heat; stir in hot pepper sauce and coconut.

Arrange ribs in a baking pan and brush generously with the sauce. Broil under preheated broiler 8 minutes, turn and broil 8 minutes more. Brush frequently with the sauce to keep the ribs moist. Arrange on a platter; serve hot. *Makes 6 servings.*

HOLIDAY SUCKLING PIG

We wish you a Merry Christmas—and a happy suntan. Roast suckling pig is the preferred holiday dish for entertaining on most islands, more than making up for the noticeable absence of snow.

4 or 5 large yams or sweet potatoes, peeled
3 medium onions, chopped
3 green onions, chopped
1 or 2 Scotch Bonnet or jalapeño chiles, chopped
Salt and freshly ground black pepper to taste
1/2 tablespoon butter
1 (10- to 12-lb.) suckling pig
Vegetable oil
1 small yam, peeled
1 cup water
2 tomatoes, chopped
1 thyme sprig

To prepare stuffing, boil large yams about 1 hour, or until tender. Drain; mash in a large bowl. Add 1 onion, green onions, chile, salt, pepper and butter. Set aside. Preheat oven to 350F (175C). Rinse and dry the pig, then brush the outside with just enough vegetable oil to produce a slight sheen. Rub inside and out with salt and pepper. Stuff pig with yam mixture. Tie the front legs together, then repeat with the back legs. Place a peeled but uncooked yam in pig's mouth, then position pig on a rack inside a roasting pan (so skin will stay crisp).

Roast in preheated oven about 15 minutes per pound, or between 2-1/2 and 3 hours, turning it over halfway through and basting often with its own juices. Juices should run clear when the pig is pierced in thickest part. Transfer the pig to a large serving dish and keep it warm. To prepare a sauce, skim excess fat from the pan juices and pour them into a medium saucepan. Add the water, tomatoes, 2 onions, thyme, salt and pepper. Reduce the liquid over high heat, then serve in a separate bowl alongside the platter of roasted pig. *Makes 6 servings with leftovers.*

ROAST GOAT ST. VINCENT

Like the Curried Goat found on many Caribbean islands, this dish from the Windward island of St. Vincent uses goat because traditionally there was no lamb.

1-1/2 cups red wine
2 tablespoons olive oil
1 large onion, sliced
6 garlic cloves, crushed
1 leg or shoulder of goat
6 medium carrots, cut into serving pieces
6 medium potatoes, cut into serving pieces
1 tablespoon guava jelly

Combine wine, olive oil, onion and garlic in a large pan. Add meat; marinate 2 hours, turning often. Preheat oven to 400F (205C). Place meat in a roasting pan. Strain marinade and pour about half the liquid into the bottom of the roasting pan; add carrots and potatoes.

Roast in preheated oven 20 minutes per pound plus 20 minutes more. Transfer the roast to a large serving dish and surround with vegetables. Spoon off grease from pan juices, then stir in the remaining marinade, scraping the browned bits from the bottom of the pan. Transfer the liquid to a saucepan; bring to a boil. Stir in the guava jelly. Serve the sauce in a bowl alongside the roast and vegetables. *Makes 4 servings.*

GRILLED LAMB CHOPS

This spectacular main dish, with its contrast of thick grilled chops against a golden sauce, can be prepared on an outdoor grill or simply done under the broiler.

1 onion, chopped
1 celery stalk, chopped
1 carrot, chopped
1 thyme sprig
1 garlic clove, crushed
1 cup red wine vinegar
1-1/2 cups vegetable oil
Salt and freshly ground black pepper to taste
4 double-thick lamb chops (cut with 2 ribs each)
1/4 cup Mango Chutney (page 21)
2 cups guava nectar
Curry powder to taste
About 1/2 teaspoon cornstarch

Combine onion, celery, carrot, thyme, garlic, vinegar, oil, salt and pepper in a large glass bowl. Add lamb chops; cover and marinate overnight in the refrigerator. If grilling outdoors, use kasha wood (available in the Caribbean) or hickory.

Preheat grill or broiler. Cook chops over the hottest part of the grill 3 to 4 minutes on each side, then move them to more moderate heat 3 to 4 minutes more per side. To prepare the chops indoors, cook them on a rack under preheated broiler 7 minutes per side. To prepare sauce, combine mango chutney, guava nectar and curry powder in a saucepan; reduce by half. Dissolve cornstarch in a little cold water. Stir into reduced sauce until thickened. To serve, cover the bottom of 2 warmed dinner plates with the sauce and position 2 chops on each. *Makes 2 servings*.

CURRIED GOAT

Don't turn up your nose at goat until you've tried it—it's actually milder tasting than lamb. Of course, if you can't find goat in your supermarket, you can substitute lamb in this classic Caribbean dish. After all, Indians immigrating to the islands chose goat after failing to find the lamb they used back home.

2 tablespoons vegetable oil
1-1/2 pounds boneless goat meat, cut into 1-inch cubes
3 large onions, diced
1 garlic clove, crushed
2 tomatoes, chopped
2 teaspoons ground allspice
2 teaspoons Curry Powder (page 27), or favorite commercial curry powder
3 cups Chicken Stock (page 23)
1 tablespoon wine vinegar
Salt and red (cayenne) pepper to taste
1/2 bay leaf
Cooked white rice

Heat oil in a Dutch oven over medium heat. Add meat in batches; cook until browned. Remove with a slotted spoon. Add onions, garlic and tomatoes; cook until soft but not brown. Stir in allspice and curry powder. Cook, stirring, about 3 minutes, then add stock, vinegar, salt and cayenne. Return meat to pan and simmer slowly 1-1/2 hours. Add bay leaf; cook about 30 minutes. Remove bay leaf before serving. Serve with rice. *Makes 6 servings.*

SUNDAY ROAST BEEF

This is Sunday dinner in many households around the islands. It is particularly beloved for its dark rich gravy, given pungency by Scotch Bonnet and Pickapeppa Sauce.

1 (5-lb.) boneless beef roast
4 teaspoons salt
1 teaspoon pepper
1 sprig fresh thyme
2 green onions, chopped
2 Scotch Bonnet chiles, chopped
2 tablespoons minced garlic
2 tablespoons Pickapeppa Sauce
2 tablespoons vegetable oil
Water

Slice into the beef and fill the openings with the seasonings. Tie the roast to keep its shape. Cover and refrigerate overnight.

Heat oil in a Dutch oven. Add the beef and brown on all sides. Add about 1/2 cup water and simmer, covered, adding only small amounts of water through the cooking process. Simmer, covered, about 4 hours total or until the meat can be cut easily with a fork. Serve with the cooking juices. *Makes 8 to 10 servings.*

BROWN STEW BEEF

As with Brown Stew Fish, this is a simple way to produce the intensity of flavor Jamaicans adore, along with the gravy they love to sop up with anything that's handy. The gravy should be a glorious reddish brown.

3 pounds lean beef, cubed
Salt and freshly ground black pepper
1 tablespoon minced garlic
1 Scotch Bonnet chile, minced
2 sprigs fresh thyme
2 tablespoons Pickapeppa Sauce
1 large onion, sliced
1 green bell pepper, sliced
3 plum tomatoes, chopped
3 green onions, chopped
1/4 cup vegetable oil
3 carrots sliced
1/2 chayote, sliced
3 to 4 cups water
4 large potatoes, halved
1/2 cup dry red wine

In a glass dish, mix the beef cubes with salt, black pepper, chile, thyme, Pickapeppa Sauce, sliced onion, bell pepper, tomatoes and green onions. Cover and marinate 1 hour in the refrigerator.

Heat the oil in a Dutch oven over medium-high heat. Add beef, a few cubes at a time, and cook until browned. When all are browned, return beef and marinating ingredients to the Dutch oven along with the carrots and chayote. Add water. Cover and simmer, about 1 hour or until beef is almost tender. Add the potatoes and wine and simmer about 20 minutes or until beef and vegetables are tender. *Makes 6 servings.*

STEW PEAS & RICE

In this national dish, enough meat is used to turn a vegetable into a main course. Though it is always served over fluffy white rice, the flour dumplings known on the island as spinners tend to be added—making the dish even more filling.

1/2 pound pig's tail
1/2 pound salt beef
2 pounds shin of beef
2 cups red kidney beans, rinsed
Water
1 sprig fresh thyme
2 cloves garlic, crushed
2 green onions, chopped
2 Scotch Bonnet chiles, chopped
Salt and freshly ground black pepper to taste
Spinners (page 72)

Soak the first two meats in cold water 1 hour and drain. Cut salt beef in small pieces. Place the beans in a large pan and add the meats with enough water to cover. Bring to a boil, then reduce the heat to low. Simmer, covered, until the meats are tender, about 2 hours, adding water as necessary. The beans should be starting to break apart. Add the seasonings, tasting before adding any salt. Stir in the Spinners and serve very hot over white rice.   *Makes 6 to 8 servings.*

COWFOOT & BEANS

Here is one of several recipes Jamaicans like to use for pieces of meat that would otherwise be ignored. The result is delicious.

1 whole cowfoot
2 medium onions, chopped
2 garlic cloves, chopped
2 tomatoes, chopped
2 green onions, chopped
1 sprig fresh thyme
1 Scotch Bonnet chile, sliced
3 tablespoons Curry Powder (page 27)
1/2 pound cooked broad beans
Salt and freshly ground black pepper to taste

Have the butcher cut the cow's foot in small pieces. Place pieces in a large heavy saucepan, cover with water and simmer until tender, 2-1/2 to 3 hours. Remove the bones and discard. Leave just enough liquid in the pan to make a gravy. Add onions, garlic, tomatoes, green onions, thyme, chile and curry powder, cover and simmer until the liquid begins to thicken. Add the cooked beans and simmer 10 minutes. Season to taste with salt and pepper. *Makes 4 servings.*

VEGETABLES

Vegetables have always been special to the Caribbean cook. Even the earliest European explorers, their ships loaded with cuttings and seeds from the Old World, found a wealth of tropical wonders already flourishing when they arrived. With the addition of their new crops, the Caribbean was paradise indeed. When it comes to vegetables, the most important thing that can be said about island cooks is that they have little patience with new ways of cooking that keep the ingredients nearly raw and banish all sauces to some allegedly unhealthy netherland. Islanders are always willing to give away a few vitamins in return for the deep flavors vegetables take on when slowly simmered, smothered or stewed. Caribbean people really love their vegetables—with meat or without.

White Rice with Tomatoes

In the old days, no island cook worth his skillet would have used the French term *concasse*. Yet that is pretty much what he would make of the tomatoes before mixing them with the rice.

6 tablespoons butter or margarine
1 medium onion, finely chopped
1-1/2 cups uncooked rice
3 cups water
2 teaspoons salt
3 medium tomatoes, peeled, seeded, diced

Melt 4 tablespoons butter over medium heat. Add onion; cook about 1 minute, then stir in rice. Add water and salt, bring to a boil and reduce heat. Cover and cook 15 to 20 minutes, until water is absorbed. When rice is cooked, melt remaining butter in a separate saucepan. Add tomatoes; cook 15 to 20 seconds. Stir into rice. *Makes 6 servings.*

RICE & PEAS

From Coat of Arms in Jamaica to Moros y Cristianos in Cuba, this is a true Caribbean standard. Rice & Peas can be served with virtually any combination of island dishes—and it usually is.

1 cup kidney beans, soaked overnight
1 quart Coconut Milk (page 26)
1 garlic clove, minced
2 green onions, finely chopped
1 thyme sprig, finely chopped
3 cups uncooked rice
2 teaspoons salt
1 tablespoon sugar

In a medium saucepan, mix soaked beans and coconut milk; cook over medium heat until tender but not mushy. Add garlic, onions, thyme, rice, salt and sugar. Cook, covered, over medium heat, stirring once or twice, until rice reaches desired texture. Add additional water if necessary. *Makes 6 servings.*

CURRY RICE

This Indian-inspired rice makes a wonderful companion to many preparations of chicken or fish.

1-1/2 cups long-grain rice
3 cups water
2 teaspoons salt
1 teaspoon Curry Powder (page 27), or favorite commercial curry powder

Place all ingredients in a medium saucepan over medium heat, cover and cook until water has evaporated, about 20 minutes. *Makes 6 servings.*

VARIATION

Stir in 1/2 cup raisins or 1/2 cup flaked coconut when rice is almost dry.

SAFFRON RICE

Of classic Spanish origin, this rice made an early crossing to the Caribbean and opted to stay. You'll find it popular even on islands with little or no link to Spain.

2 tablespoons butter or margarine
1/2 small onion, finely chopped
1-1/2 cups water
1/2 teaspoon salt
1 cup long-grain rice
1/2 teaspoon powdered saffron

Melt butter in a medium saucepan with a tight-fitting lid. Add onion; cook until soft. Add the water and salt. Bring to a boil; stir in rice. Stir in saffron. Bring to a boil again, stir and cover. Simmer 15 minutes, then uncover and continue cooking until rice is tender and fluffy. *Makes 6 servings.*

Eggplant Port-au-Prince

The eggplant, also known as *aubergine* on French islands or garden-egg in Jamaica, came into the Caribbean with the Portuguese Jews. It was adopted most readily into the Creole cooking of Haiti, where this recipe is a favorite.

2 large eggplants
3 tablespoons olive oil
4 dry bread slices
1/4 cup milk
3 eggs
6 green onions, sliced in 1/2-inch rounds
2 tablespoons freshly chopped parsley
2 garlic cloves, minced
1 tablespoon fresh basil, finely chopped
1 dash hot pepper sauce
1 teaspoon grated lemon peel
Salt and freshly ground black pepper to taste
About 1 cup Chicken Stock (page 23)

Lemon Sauce

1 cup Chicken Stock (page 23)
8 egg yolks
1/4 cup freshly squeezed lemon juice
White pepper to taste

Grease a large baking dish; set aside. Preheat oven to 375F (190C). Cut eggplants in half lengthwise. Heat olive oil in a large skillet. Slash cut sides of eggplants several times, then place cut-side-down in oil, cover and cook 10 minutes. Scoop out pulp, leaving shells about 1/4 inch thick. Set shells aside. Chop eggplant pulp, add to skillet and cook 5 minutes.

In a large bowl, moisten bread with milk and mix thoroughly with eggs. Stir in cooked pulp, onions, parsley, garlic, basil, hot pepper sauce, lemon peel, salt and black pepper. Stuff eggplant shells with mixture and place them in greased baking dish. Pour in chicken stock to about 1/4 inch deep and bake in preheated oven 30 to 35 minutes. Make sauce while eggplants are baking. *Makes 8 servings.*

LEMON SAUCE

With a whisk, beat all sauce ingredients together in a round-bottomed saucepan set over hot water over medium heat until sauce gets thick and frothy. Remove from heat immediately; overcooking will diminish fluffiness. Serve in a bowl alongside stuffed eggplants. *Makes 8 servings.*

GREEN BANANA CEVICHE

The Spaniards' love affair with pickling finds its way into meat and fish dishes on virtually every island. Here it makes for a colorful side dish.

10 small green bananas
3 tablespoons salt
2 cups olive oil
1 cup white vinegar
12 black peppercorns
1/2 teaspoon salt
2 bay leaves
3 medium onions, thinly sliced
2 garlic cloves, minced

To prepare bananas, trim ends and make a slit in peel on either side of each banana. Do not remove peel or cut into banana itself. Place in a pot with enough water to cover and bring to a boil. Simmer 15 minutes, drain and peel.

Bring 2 quarts of water and the 3 tablespoons salt to a boil. Add peeled bananas and boil 15 minutes; drain and cool. To prepare sauce, stir together all remaining ingredients in a heavy skillet; cook over low heat 1 hour. To assemble dish, cut bananas into 1-inch rounds and layer in a deep dish with sauce. Let marinate, refrigerated, 24 hours before serving. *Makes 8 servings.*

CALLALOO

If Popeye the Sailor hailed from the Caribbean, he'd no doubt spring open a can of callaloo whenever he needed a lift. This version especially is quite a bit more memorable than spinach.

3 pounds fresh callaloo or kale
6 cups water
1 cup chopped celery
1 cup chopped onion
1/2 cup chopped green bell pepper
1 tablespoon sugar
2 garlic cloves, minced
1 or 2 Scotch Bonnet or jalapeño chiles

Using a sharp knife, cut away any bruised or blemished spots on callaloo. Wash leaves in cold running water, until all traces of dirt and sand are removed. Cut up callaloo and combine in a Dutch oven with all remaining ingredients. Cover and bring to a boil, reduce heat and cook until tender, about 1 hour. *Makes 6 servings.*

MT. DIABLO GRILLED CORN

Mt. Diablo in Jamaica is about halfway between Kingston and north coast playgrounds like Ocho Rios. Since most people making the drive hit Mt. Diablo about noontime, dozens of ramshackle food stalls have sprung up. My favorite entrepreneurs are those hawking this peppery grilled corn.

6 ears fresh corn
1 Scotch Bonnet or jalapeño chile
1 tablespoon black peppercorns
1 thyme sprig
1 rosemary sprig
1 garlic clove
1/2 teaspoon salt

Preheat grill. Pull down (but do not tear off) husks and remove silks, then replace husks. Soak corn with husks in cold water 30 minutes. While corn is soaking, prepare a paste by crushing chile, peppercorns, thyme, rosemary, garlic and salt with a mortar. Remove corn from water, pull back husks again and spread paste over kernels by hand. Replace husks. Arrange corn on hot grill and cook, turning often, about 20 minutes. Pull off husks and serve hot. *Makes 6 servings*.

STEWED PINK BEANS

This dish, which can be made with virtually any dry bean, demonstrates the importance Puerto Rico and other Latin islands attach to *sofrito*. Derived from the Spanish verb *sofreír* (meaning to fry lightly), it is an essential flavor element and can be prepared in large amounts and stored for two to three days in the refrigerator.

1 pound dry small pink beans
1/2 pound West Indian pumpkin (calabaza) or other pumpkin,
    peeled, cut into 1/2-inch cubes
1/2 pound white potatoes, peeled, cut into 1/2-inch cubes
Sofrito (see below)
4 tomatoes, peeled, seeded
1 Scotch Bonnet or jalapeño chile
About 1 tablespoon white vinegar
Salt and freshly ground black pepper to taste

SOFRITO

2 tablespoons vegetable oil
1/4 cup diced salt pork
1/2 cup diced ham
1/2 teaspoon dried leaf oregano
2 medium onions, finely chopped
1 green bell pepper, finely chopped
6 garlic cloves, finely chopped
4 cilantro leaves, finely chopped

Rinse the beans in cold water, then soak overnight in water to cover. Drain beans; discard any that did not swell. Place beans and 2 quarts of cold water in a large pan; bring to a boil. Simmer 30 minutes, then add pumpkin and potatoes. Cook another 30 minutes, or until beans are almost tender.

Meanwhile make Sofrito. Mash some of pumpkin and potato against side of pan. Add Sofrito, tomatoes and chile. Cook 30 minutes more, or until liquid thickens. Add vinegar to taste. Season to taste with salt and black pepper. *Makes 6 servings.*

Sofrito

Heat oil in a large skillet over medium heat. Add salt pork and ham; cook until browned. Add the oregano; stir 30 seconds, then add remaining ingredients. Reduce heat. Cook, stirring, until onions are soft.

Peas & Fresh Okra

Whenever there is fresh okra, islanders cook it with virtually everything. They love the way it thickens as it flavors.

2 pounds fresh pigeon peas or black-eyed peas, shelled
1/2 pound salt pork, sliced
1 pound fresh okra
Salt and freshly ground black pepper to taste

Place peas in a heavy saucepan. Cover with water and add salt pork. Bring to a boil and cook 30 to 40 minutes until tender. Slice okra in 1/4-inch rounds and place on top of cooked peas.

Cover saucepan and remove it from heat, allowing okra to cook in steam from peas until crisp-tender. Season with salt and black pepper. *Makes 6 servings.*

ACCRA

Pounding, grinding and crushing were essential cooking skills in West Africa, and they came to the Caribbean with the slaves. Few dishes could be simpler, earthier or more traditional than Accra, also known as Calas in the Dutch islands.

4 cups dried black-eyed peas
12 Scotch Bonnet or jalapeño chiles
Salt to taste
Vegetable oil for frying

Soak peas overnight; drain. Rub off skins, then soak peas an additional 2 hours. Crush chiles in a mortar and transfer them to a large bowl. Drain peas, then crush them in a mortar until they are free of lumps. Add peas to chiles and beat with a wooden spoon until mixture is light and fluffy. Season with salt.

Heat oil to smoking in a heavy skillet, then drop pea-chile mixture into oil by spoonfuls. Fry, in batches, until golden brown, and drain on paper towels. *Makes 6 servings*.

Corn & Sweet Pepper Sauté

Corn is often called Indian corn on the islands. Though the Indians knew nothing of sautéing, this preparation celebrates their contribution of corn while bursting with eye appeal.

4 cups corn, cut from about 8 ears
1/2 green bell pepper, diced
1/2 red bell pepper, diced
1/4 cup butter or margarine, melted
1/2 cup half and half
1/2 teaspoon salt
Freshly ground black pepper to taste

Combine corn, bell peppers and butter in a large skillet. Cover and cook over medium heat 2 minutes. Reduce heat. Add half and half, season with salt and pepper and cook, uncovered, over low heat 5 to 7 minutes more, or until liquid is absorbed. Stir frequently during cooking. *Makes 6 servings*.

Spicy Orange Carrot Sticks

Here is a bright and satisfying side dish made so by the mixture of orange juice, brown sugar and ginger.

3/4 cup orange juice
1 tablespoon light brown sugar
1/4 teaspoon ground ginger
Freshly ground black pepper to taste
6 carrots, cut in matchsticks (about 3 cups)
Chopped parsley

Combine orange juice, brown sugar, ginger, pepper and carrots in a medium saucepan. Cover and cook over medium-high heat until carrots are crisp-tender. Sprinkle parsley on top. *Makes 6 servings.*

Cou-Cou

A favorite in Barbados, cou-cou might be described as a vegetable fritter cooked in a casserole instead of hot oil. Or it might more simply be described as delightful. Variations without okra turn up as Funchi or Fungi in the Virgin Islands and the Netherlands Antilles.

2 tablespoons butter or margarine, softened
2-1/2 cups water
1 teaspoon salt
1/3 pound okra, cut into 1/4-inch-thick rounds
1 cup yellow cornmeal
1 dash hot pepper sauce

Rub about half the butter over the inside of a shallow, 3-cup heatproof dish. In a heavy saucepan, bring the water and salt to a boil. Add okra and boil until tender, about 10 minutes, then remove with a slotted spoon. Return water to a boil, reduce heat to low and stir in cornmeal in a slow, steady stream. Stir in okra in two batches and continue stirring until a thick mixture forms, about 5 minutes. Stir in hot pepper sauce and spoon mixture into buttered dish. Spread remaining butter over top and serve immediately. *Makes 4 servings.*

CURRIED BANANAS

Most Americans don't think of serving bananas as a vegetable. All the same, with a dash of curry, they make a wonderful accompaniment to meat or fish.

6 large ripe bananas
1/4 cup butter or margarine
1 tablespoon Curry Powder (page 27), or favorite commercial curry powder

Peel bananas and slice into 1/4-inch-thick rounds. Melt butter in a large skillet; stir in curry powder, cooking about 2 minutes. Add bananas; cook until lightly browned, about 7 minutes. *Makes 6 servings.*

SKILLET TOMATOES

Simple and direct—two words that say so much about the method of Caribbean cooking as well as its special character on the plate. When tomatoes are fresh and flavorful, who could ask for anything more?

4 medium tomatoes
3 tablespoons butter or margarine
1 medium onion, cut in rings
1 small garlic clove, minced
1 teaspoon salt
1 teaspoon dried leaf basil
Freshly ground black pepper to taste

Remove stems from tomatoes, then cut each into 6 to 8 wedges and set aside. Melt butter in a large skillet, add onion and garlic and cook over medium-high heat 2 minutes. Stir in salt, basil and black pepper. Add reserved tomatoes to skillet, reduce heat to medium and stir just until hot, 2 to 3 minutes. *Makes 6 servings.*

Candied Sweet Potatoes

If your taste in vegetables runs to the sweet, you won't be alone in the Caribbean. With their sweet tooth inherited from the English, islanders even add syrup to this dish on occasion.

2 pounds sweet potatoes
1/4 cup butter or margarine
1/4 teaspoon freshly grated nutmeg
1/2 cup water

Preheat oven to 350F (175C). Butter a 2-quart casserole dish. Boil sweet potatoes in lightly salted water in a large saucepan until they are tender. Drain potatoes and cool slightly. Peel and slice potatoes 1/4 to 1/2 inch thick. Arrange slices in layers in buttered casserole dish, dotting each layer with butter and sprinkling with nutmeg. Add water and bake in preheated oven until top is crisp, about 45 minutes.   *Makes 6 servings*.

BREADS

"Fry fish and bammy!" "Fry fish and bammy!"
That is their cry, these bandannaed, seemingly
ancient women peddling their wares to pass-
ing cars along many an island coastal road. Actually, by pairing bammy with the crispy fried
fish in their "show cases," the women are
keeping alive a tradition of breadmaking that
goes back as far as the Arawaks. The oh-so-
typical cassava bread, originally known as
zabi, has somehow sauntered through the centuries to appear as sidekick to many Caribbean
dishes.

Breads leavened with yeast came considerably later in island history—and they failed
to become common due to the short life span

of fresh yeast in the days before refrigeration. Even with commercial white bread available today, islanders opt for a dense bread they call "hard dough." Breads in the Caribbean also encompass corn breads similar to those of the American South and baked goods sweetened with tropical fruits such as the ever-present banana.

CARIBBEAN JOHNNYCAKE

Traditionally, Caribbean breakfasts were hearty affairs, complete with meat, fish and plenty of fruit. Even though breakfasts tend to be lighter now, islanders still love these hot johnnycakes.

2 cups all-purpose flour
2 tablespoons baking powder
1/4 teaspoon salt
1 teaspoon sugar
1 tablespoon vegetable shortening
About 1/2 cup water
1/2 cup vegetable oil

Sift together flour, baking powder, salt and sugar into a medium bowl. Cut in shortening until mixture resembles cornmeal. Add water a little at a time to make a sticky dough. Knead dough until smooth, adding additional flour if needed. On a floured board, shape dough into a long roll 1-1/2 to 2 inches across. Cut dough into 1-inch pieces and roll each into a small ball, then flatten each gently by hand or with a floured rolling pin.

Heat oil over medium heat in a medium skillet. Fry johnnycakes, in batches, until they are golden on both sides. Remove and drain on paper towels. Serve hot. *Makes about 12 johnnycakes.*

Coconut-Banana Cornbread

As we see in this recipe and the one that follows, cornbread in the Caribbean ranges from sweet to savory.

1 cup yellow cornmeal
1 cup all-purpose flour
1 tablespoon sugar
1 tablespoon baking powder
1-1/4 teaspoons ground allspice
1/4 teaspoon salt
1 egg, beaten
1 cup mashed very ripe bananas (about 2 medium)
1/4 cup milk
1/4 cup vegetable oil
1/2 cup sweetened flaked coconut

Preheat oven to 375F (190C). Grease an 8-inch square pan; set aside. In a medium bowl, combine cornmeal, flour, sugar, baking powder, allspice and salt. In another medium bowl, combine egg, bananas, milk and oil. Form a well in center of dry ingredients, add milk mixture all at once and stir just enough to combine. Stir in coconut. Pour mixture into greased pan.

Bake in preheated oven about 25 minutes or until a cake tester inserted in center comes out clean. Cut into 2-inch squares and serve hot with butter. *Makes 16 squares*.

Variation

Bake in a greased 9-inch round pan. Cut in wedges.

Sweet Pepper Cornbread

The chile adds a welcome bit of fire, not to mention contributing green to the bits of red bell pepper.

1 cup all-purpose flour
1 cup yellow cornmeal
1 tablespoon baking powder
1/2 teaspoon salt
2 large eggs
1 cup buttermilk
1/4 cup butter, melted
2 tablespoons honey
1 to 2 Scotch Bonnet or jalapeño chiles, minced
1 cup finely chopped red bell pepper

Preheat oven to 400F (205C). Grease a 9-inch square pan; set aside. In a medium bowl, combine flour, cornmeal, baking powder and salt. In another medium bowl, lightly beat the eggs, then stir in the buttermilk, butter and honey. Form a well in center of dry ingredients, add milk mixture all at once and stir just enough to combine. Stir in chile and bell pepper. Spoon batter into greased pan.

Bake in preheated oven 20 minutes, or until a cake tester inserted in center comes out clean. Place on a wire rack. Cool 10 minutes, then cut into squares and remove from pan. Serve warm.   *Makes 12 squares.*

BANANA LOAF

The mashed banana and crushed peanuts make for a nice texture contrast in this somewhat sweet bread.

1/4 pound unsalted butter
1/2 cup packed brown sugar
3 egg yolks
2 cups all-purpose flour
1 teaspoon ground cloves
1 tablespoon baking powder
1 pinch of salt
1 cup mashed very ripe bananas (about 2 medium)
1 teaspoon vanilla extract
1/2 cup chopped peanuts

Preheat oven to 325F (165C). Grease a 9 x 5-inch loaf pan; set aside. In a medium bowl, cream butter and sugar until fluffy. Add egg yolks and mix thoroughly. In another medium bowl, sift together flour, cloves, baking powder and salt.

Combine mashed banana and vanilla, then add this a little at a time to egg-butter mixture, alternating with additions of sifted dry ingredients. Beat lightly until everything is blended, then add peanuts. Mix well and pour batter into greased loaf pan.

Bake in preheated oven 1 hour, or until a cake tester inserted in center comes out clean. *Makes 1 loaf.*

GINGERBREAD

The English have always loved their gingerbread, and they never found more pungent ginger than they did in the Caribbean.

1/2 cup molasses
1 cup sugar
1/2 cup butter
1/2 cup hot water
2 cups all-purpose flour
2 teaspoons baking powder
1/2 teaspoon salt
1 teaspoon freshly grated nutmeg
2 teaspoons grated gingerroot
1 egg, beaten

Preheat oven to 300F (150C). Grease a 9-inch square pan; line with waxed paper. In a medium saucepan over low heat, gently heat molasses, sugar and butter. Mix in hot water and set pan aside. In a medium bowl, sift together flour, baking powder, salt and nutmeg. Stir in gingerroot, then egg. Mix molasses liquid with flour mixture and pour into prepared pan. Bake 1 hour, or until a cake tester inserted in center comes out clean. Cut in squares. *Makes 9 squares.*

BAMMY

As you might guess from the technique, Africans deserve most of the credit for this wonderful bread. Bammy is one of the best "street foods" in all the Caribbean, perfect for munching while strolling.

6 cups grated cassava (yucca root)
1-1/2 teaspoons salt

Grease a medium skillet. In a large bowl, mix grated cassava and salt. Place about 1 cup of mixture in greased skillet. Press down (islanders often use bottom of a bottle) until bammies are about 6 inches in diameter.

Place skillet over medium heat. When steam starts to rise and bammy's edge shrinks slightly from side of pan, press mixture flat again and turn it. Cook about 5 minutes per side. Repeat process with remaining cassava-salt mixture. Serve hot or cool and store, tightly wrapped, in the refrigerator up to 4 days—or freeze until needed.

To serve later, soak bammies in milk about 10 minutes. Fry them in a bit of oil until outside starts to brown, butter them and serve hot. *Makes 6 servings*.

EASTER BUNS

Remember that childhood rhyme about Hot Cross Buns? Well, the English brought both rhyme and bun when they moved into the Caribbean. Islanders, who don't have much to mark the seasons, consider these Easter treats the best part of Spring.

1 (1/4-oz.) package dry yeast (about 1 tablespoon)
1/3 cup packed brown sugar
1/2 teaspoon salt
1 teaspoon ground cinnamon
1 teaspoon freshly grated nutmeg
4 cups all-purpose flour
1/4 cup butter
1 cup milk
2 eggs
1/4 cup raisins
1/4 cup currants
1/4 cup chopped red candied cherries
1/2 egg mixed with 1 tablespoon milk
1/4 cup powdered sugar
2 teaspoons water

Mix yeast, sugar, salt, cinnamon and nutmeg with 1 cup of flour in a large bowl. Melt butter in a small saucepan, add milk and heat until very warm. Add this to flour mixture and beat until smooth. Add the eggs, and 1 more cup of flour, beating until very smooth and scraping down side of bowl. Gradually add rest of flour until a soft dough is formed. Turn dough onto a floured board and knead until smooth and elastic, about 10 minutes. Grease a large bowl. Place dough in greased bowl, turning it once to coat the surface. Cover and let rise 1 hour in a warm place, until dough doubles in bulk.

Punch down dough and add raisins, currants and cherries, kneading to distribute them throughout dough. Divide dough into halves, then shape each half into an 8-inch square. Cut each square into 9 pieces. Grease 2 (9-inch) baking pans. Place each set of buns in a greased pan, cover and let rise in a warm place 1 hour.

Preheat oven to 375F (190C). While it is heating, cut a cross in top of each bun and brush with egg-milk mixture. Bake in preheated oven 15 to 20 minutes or until brown. Mix powdered sugar and 2 teaspoons water in a small bowl. Frost buns while they are still slightly warm. *Makes 18 buns.*

BAKES

In Trinidad and Tobago, these are the breads in which you wrap the fried shark to produce Shark & Bake. Bakes are good, however, all by themselves.

2 cups all-purpose flour
2 teaspoons baking powder
1 teaspoon salt
8 tablespoons butter
1 teaspoon sugar
About 3/4 cup water
About 1 tablespoon vegetable oil

Sift together the flour, baking powder and salt in a large bowl, then cut in the butter until mixture resembles coarse crumbs. Stir in sugar. Stir in enough water to make a soft dough. Knead dough gently on a lightly floured surface. Cut into 4 to 6 pieces and roll each piece into a ball. Let stand 5 minutes.

Flatten the balls to 1/4-inch-thick rounds. Heat oil in a skillet. Add rounds and cook until golden brown, turning. Drain on paper towels and serve warm.   *Makes 4 to 6 pieces.*

TURN CORNMEAL

You sometimes find this strange cornbread quite plain, but most often Jamaican cooks like to season it a little. In this recipe, we season ours more than a little.

1/4 cup vegetable oil
1 large tomato, diced
1 large green bell pepper, diced
12 okras, sliced
1 large onion, diced
1 green onion, diced
Salt and black pepper to taste
1/2 teaspoon minced garlic
1 quart water
2 cups yellow cornmeal

Heat the oil in a medium saucepan. Add vegetables and sauté until softened, then add the water and bring to a boil. Quickly add all the cornmeal and cook, stirring vigorously with a whisk, about 10 minutes. Once the mixture is combined and thickened, cover and steam over very low heat about 30 minutes. Turn onto a serving plate and cut in wedges. *Makes 6 servings.*

Festival

Traditionally served with fried fish at Hellshire Beach, this fried cornbread takes its name from the celebrations each year the first weekend in August to commemorate Jamaica's independence. It is terrific with many of the dishes in this book.

1 cup yellow cornmeal
3/4 cup all-purpose flour
1/4 cup light brown sugar
1 teaspoon baking powder
1/2 teaspoon salt
1 egg
About 1 cup water
Vegetable oil for deep-frying

Mix the dry ingredients together in a medium bowl. Beat the egg lightly with the water in a small bowl. Add to the cornmeal mixture and stir into a soft dough.

Heat oil in a deep heavy saucepan to 375F (19OC) or until a 1-inch bread cube turns golden brown in 50 seconds. Tear off pieces of dough; roll into ovals in your hands. Add to hot oil and cook until golden brown. Drain on paper towels. Serve warm.   *Makes 4 servings.*

DESSERTS

The French, Spanish and Portuguese all brought rich dessert traditions to the Caribbean—flaky pastries, creamy puddings, sweets from simple to sophisticated. Yet even many of these cooks would concede they had less to do with the Caribbean's insatiable sweet tooth than the English. From Jamaica all the way down to Barbados, explorers and colonists from Great Britain convinced islanders of nearly every ethnic persuasion that cakes, pies and tarts were the highlight of any meal. They also convinced islanders that miniature versions of these delights made perfect snacks while waiting for the bus or the mail boat. As a result, most candid paintings or photographs of Caribbean people seem to include at least one man, woman or child munching on an enticing pastry.

SPONGE CAKE

Here is a good basic cake that is used, in different shapes, for both the Trifle and the Calypso Cake.

3 large eggs
1/2 cup superfine sugar
1/2 cup sifted cake flour
1/4 teaspoon salt
1/4 cup clarified butter
1/2 teaspoon vanilla extract

Preheat oven to 350F (175C). Grease bottom and side of a 9-inch round pan, then line bottom with waxed paper and grease the paper. Put a tablespoon of flour in pan and shake it around to coat, pouring out any excess. To make cake, combine eggs and sugar in top of a double boiler over hot water. Set double boiler over low heat, beating mixture about 15 minutes, until very thick and pale, and it falls in a thick ribbon when whisk is lifted. Pour mixture into a medium bowl.

Sift together flour and salt onto a piece of waxed paper. Sprinkle 1/4 of the flour mixture over egg-sugar mixture and fold in with a rubber spatula. Fold in remaining flour mixture, then add butter and vanilla about 1/3 at a time. Turn batter immediately into prepared pan and smooth top gently with rubber spatula. Bake 25 to 30 minutes, or until top of cake springs back when pressed with your fingertip. Cool on a wire rack 15 minutes, then turn cake out onto rack. If waxed paper sticks to cake, remove it carefully. Cool. *Makes 1 (9-inch) cake.*

BANANA MUFFINS

This recipe from chef Gerard Messerli at the Hyatt Regency Cerromar Beach in Puerto Rico makes 12 extra-large muffins with a crunchy cinnamon sugar topping. For rich banana flavor, use very ripe bananas.

2 cups all-purpose flour
2-1/2 teaspoons baking powder
1/2 teaspoon salt
1/2 cup butter, softened
1 cup plus 1 tablespoon sugar
2 eggs
1 teaspoon vanilla extract
1-1/2 cups mashed very ripe bananas (about 2 bananas)
1/4 cup milk
1/2 teaspoon ground cinnamon

Preheat oven to 375F (190C). Butter 12 extra-large muffin cups. Sift flour, baking powder and salt together. Set aside. In a large bowl with an electric mixer at medium speed, cream butter and 1 cup of sugar until light and fluffy. Add eggs 1 at a time, then beat in vanilla. Combine bananas and milk in a small bowl. On low speed, stir flour into egg mixture alternately with bananas, stirring just until combined. Spoon into greased muffin cups.

Combine remaining 1 tablespoon of sugar and cinnamon in a small bowl. Sprinkle over muffins. Bake in preheated oven 30 minutes, or until wooden pick inserted in center comes out clean. Cool in pan 5 minutes. *Makes 12 extra-large muffins.*

Calypso Cake

If calypso is to many the musical embodiment of the Caribbean, this cake might be called the islands captured in confection.

1 Sponge Cake (page 172), baked in a tube pan, cooled
1/2 pint (1 cup) whipping cream
3/4 cup coconut rum
5 cups chopped mixed tropical fruit (orange, mango, papaya, pineapple)
Mint for garnish

Invert cooled cake onto a serving plate. Using a long serrated knife, cut a circle around top of cake about an inch from outer edge and about 2/3 of way down through cake. Working from cut circle to center hole, lift out wedges of cake. Use wedges to line center hole so cake forms a container.

Just before serving, whip cream and 1/4 cup coconut rum in a chilled medium bowl until mixture is stiff. Fold another 1/4 cup rum into whipped cream mixture, then sprinkle remaining rum over cake. Reserve 1 cup of mixed fruit for garnish. Gently fold remaining fruit into whipped cream. Spoon cream mixture into center of cake. Garnish with reserved fruit and mint. Serve immediately. *Makes 12 to 14 servings.*

LIME PIE

This pie has over the years made its way as far north as the Florida Keys, where it became key lime pie.

1 cup sugar
2 tablespoons all-purpose flour
3 tablespoons cornstarch
1/4 teaspoon salt
2 cups boiling water
3 egg yolks, beaten
3/4 cup freshly squeezed lime juice
1 teaspoon grated lime peel
1 tablespoon butter
1 (9-inch) Pie Crust (page 182), baked
3 egg whites
3 tablespoons sugar

Blend 1 cup sugar, flour, cornstarch and salt in top of a double boiler over hot water, then stir in boiling water and cook, stirring, until mixture thickens. Continue cooking over low heat 10 minutes, then remove from heat. Stir a small amount of hot mixture into egg yolks. Whisk into hot mixture and cook, stirring, 2 minutes. Add lime juice, grated peel and butter. Pour into crust.

Preheat oven to 350F (175C). To prepare meringue, beat egg whites in a medium bowl until stiff but not dry, adding sugar a little at a time. Spoon meringue over top of pie and bake in preheated oven just until top starts to brown. Refrigerate until chilled. *Makes 1 pie, 8 servings.*

Plantain Tarts

Tarts are always popular on islands with an English legacy. It's hard to spot an islander waiting for anything without a wonderful fruit tart in his hand.

Pastry

2 cups all-purpose flour
1 cup vegetable shortening
1 teaspoon ground cinnamon
1/4 teaspoon freshly grated nutmeg
1/4 teaspoon salt
About 2 tablespoons ice water

Filling

1 cup mashed very ripe plantain
1/2 cup sugar
1 tablespoon butter
1/2 teaspoon freshly grated nutmeg
1 teaspoon vanilla extract
1 tablespoon raisins

Pastry

Combine half the flour with the shortening in a medium bowl and cut in with a pastry blender until mixture resembles peas. Add remaining flour, cinnamon, nutmeg and salt. Again, cut in until mixture resembles bread crumbs. Add enough ice water to hold mixture together, then form in a ball, wrap and refrigerate 1 to 2 hours.

Filling

Combine plantain, sugar and butter in a saucepan and cook thoroughly over low heat. Remove from heat, then stir in nutmeg, vanilla and raisins. Let filling cool.

To complete

Preheat oven to 450F (230C). Turn dough out on a lightly floured board and roll to 1/8-inch thickness. Cut dough into 4-inch circles and spoon some of filling into center of each. Fold dough over filling and seal by crimping edges with a fork. Place tarts on a baking sheet. Prick top of each tart with a fork and bake 30 minutes, or until pastry is delicately brown. *Makes 6 servings.*

MATRIMONY

A lovely dessert with a lovely name, this is an island favorite.

6 large starfruit (carambola)
4 oranges
1 (14-oz.) can sweetened condensed milk
Nutmeg
Sugar

To prepare starfruit, cut off bottoms less than halfway down, revealing shape that gives fruit its name. Scoop out soft pulp, then pick out and discard seeds. Peel oranges, cut them into sections. Mix starfruit and oranges, then refrigerate until dish is served. Stir in milk. Grate a bit of nutmeg over top and sweeten to taste with sugar. *Makes 6 servings.*

Banana Puffs with Coffee-Rum Sauce

~~~~~🌴~~~~~

I could enjoy just about anything (especially these wonderful banana puffs) in this sauce, which showcases two of the Caribbean's most significant exports.

Puffs

1 cup water
1 cup butter
1/8 teaspoon salt
2 cups all-purpose flour
8 eggs

Cream Filling

1 pint (2 cups) whipping cream
1 to 2 tablespoons banana extract, to taste
Sugar, to taste

Coffee-Rum Sauce

1 cup sugar
1-1/2 cups hot coffee
3 tablespoons cold coffee
2 tablespoons cornstarch
2 tablespoons butter
2 tablespoons rum

Puffs

Preheat oven to 400F (205C). Lightly grease a baking sheet. Bring water to a boil in a heavy medium saucepan, then add butter and salt. Stir, reduce heat and add flour, beating mixture until it pulls away from side of pan to form a smooth ball in center. Remove from heat and add eggs 1 at a time, beating well after each addition.

Using a spoon, shape puffs into 1-1/2-inch balls and place them on greased baking sheet. Bake in preheated oven 8 minutes, then reduce heat to 350F (175C) and bake an additional 10 to 12 minutes, until golden brown. Cool on wire racks.

CREAM FILLING

Mix cream and banana extract in a chilled medium bowl. Whip mixture until soft peaks form. Beat in sugar to taste.

COFFEE-RUM SAUCE

Melt sugar in a heavy medium saucepan over low heat while stirring constantly. Gradually add the hot coffee, stirring until sugar is completely dissolved.

In a separate bowl, mix cold coffee and cornstarch, then combine this with heated mixture. Cook until mixture comes to a boil and thickens. Remove from heat, add butter and rum and stir until butter melts.

TO COMPLETE

Fill cooled puffs with cream filling. Place filled puffs on serving dishes. Top with warm sauce. *Makes 6 to 8 servings.*

TROPICAL FRUITS WITH CHOCOLATE

Fruits are more traditional in the Caribbean than chocolate, but there are chocoholics here as well. This fun presentation blends both forms of sweet.

1 (15-oz.) can cream of coconut
12 ounces good-quality semisweet or bittersweet chocolate, finely chopped
Tropical fruits (starfruit, papaya, mango, pineapple), cut in chunks
    (about 4 cups)

Combine cream of coconut and chocolate in top of a double boiler over hot but not simmering water. Stir until chocolate is melted and smooth, then pour sauce into a chafing dish.

Arrange prepared fruits on a serving platter and use fondue forks or wooden picks to dip them into sauce, which should be kept warm. *Makes 8 servings.*

BAKED BANANAS

For old-fashioned good taste, it's hard to beat this island classic.

6 large, firm ripe bananas
1/2 cup dark rum
1/3 cup butter, melted
1/3 cup packed light brown sugar
3/4 teaspoon ground allspice
1/4 cup lemon juice
Vanilla ice cream, if desired

Preheat oven to 375F (190C). Grease a 1-1/2- to 2-quart casserole dish. Peel bananas and slice in half crosswise, then place in greased casserole dish.

Combine rum, butter, brown sugar, allspice and lemon juice in a small bowl and pour over bananas, turning them to coat. Cover and bake until bananas are easily pierced with a knife, about 20 minutes. Serve warm with vanilla ice cream, if desired. *Makes 6 servings.*

TEMBLEQUE

This is the Puerto Rican version of the classic Spanish dessert called flan. It is a perfect choice when something light is needed to end a meal in style.

4 cups milk
1/8 teaspoon salt
1 cup sugar
8 eggs
1 teaspoon vanilla extract
6 tablespoons sugar

Preheat oven to 300F (150C). Pour milk into a large saucepan, add salt and heat until bubbles form around edge of milk. Remove from the heat and add 1 cup sugar, stirring until it is dissolved. Set aside. In a large bowl, beat eggs until they are foamy, then gradually stir in milk-sugar mixture. Add vanilla and stir well.

Melt 6 tablespoons sugar in a small skillet until it is light golden, then use this caramel to coat a 1-1/2-quart tube pan. Pour the custard mixture into pan and place pan in a shallow pan with hot water about halfway up the sides. Bake about 1 hour or until a knife inserted in the center comes out clean. Cool thoroughly before inverting onto a shallow serving plate. *Makes 6 servings.*

PIE CRUST

This pie crust should serve you well, whatever you choose as filling.

2 cups all-purpose flour
1 pinch of salt
5 tablespoons unsalted butter
3 tablespoons shortening
About 1/3 cup ice water

    With fingers or a pastry cutter, combine flour, salt, butter and shortening in a medium bowl until mixture resembles coarse meal. Pour in just enough water to form a dough. Divide dough into 2 balls. Dust these in flour and cover with plastic wrap, then refrigerate 30 minutes.

    Roll out each ball to an 11-inch circle. Place 1 of circles in a 9-inch pie pan and crimp edge. Depending on recipe, you can use other circle as a top crust or as a separate pie crust. To use as prebaked crusts, preheat oven to 425F (205C). Bake in preheated oven about 15 minutes, or until golden brown. Or bake as recipe directs. *Makes 2 crusts.*

SWEET POTATO BALLS

Many Caribbean ingredients are cooked one way as a savory and another way as a sweet. In this recipe, sweet potatoes are given an unusual dessert treatment.

2 pounds sweet potatoes
6 cups water
1 teaspoon salt
3/4 cup Coconut Milk (page 26)
3 cups sugar
1 egg yolk
Ground cinnamon
Whole cloves

Scrub sweet potatoes and cut them into pieces. Place sweet potatoes, water and salt in a large saucepan. Boil, covered, over medium heat about 40 minutes, or until fork-tender. Drain sweet potatoes, peel and mash through a sieve into a medium bowl. Add Coconut Milk, sugar and egg yolk, mixing well with a wooden spoon. Pour mixture into a heavy saucepan and bring rapidly to a boil, stirring constantly. Reduce heat to medium and cook, stirring, until mixture separates completely from bottom and sides of pan. Remove from heat and cool slightly.

Shape portions of mixture into small balls. Dust them lightly with ground cinnamon and garnish each with a whole clove. *Makes 16 balls.*

PINE GROVE SWEET POTATO PUDDING

Marcia Thwaites, who runs Pine Grove as an inn and coffee farm in Jamaica's famed Blue Mountains, gave me this recipe for one of her guests' all-time favorites.

3 pounds sweet potatoes, grated
1/2 teaspoon freshly grated nutmeg
1-inch piece gingerroot, grated
1-1/2 cups packed brown sugar
1 teaspoon salt
1 (14-oz.) can sweetened condensed milk
1 teaspoon vanilla extract
1-1/2 cups water
1 cup butter, softened

Preheat oven to 375F (190C). Butter a 9-inch square pan. In a large bowl, mix sweet potatoes, nutmeg, gingerroot, brown sugar and salt. Combine milk, vanilla, water and butter in a medium bowl, then mix into sweet potato mixture. Pour into buttered pan. Bake 1-1/2 hours, until center is set. *Makes about 20 servings.*

Piña Colada Bread Pudding

Everyone loves bread pudding, and just about everyone makes it differently. Try this remarkable marriage of pudding with the Caribbean's favorite drink.

1 (10-ounce) day-old French bread loaf, broken into chunks
2 cups milk
1 (15-oz.) can cream of coconut
2 cups sugar
1/2 cup butter, melted
3 eggs
2 tablespoons vanilla extract
1 (8-oz.) can crushed pineapple
1 cup shredded coconut
1 cup chopped nuts, such as pecans
1 teaspoon ground cinnamon
1/2 teaspoon freshly grated nutmeg

Rum Sauce

1/2 cup butter
1-1/2 cups sugar
1 egg yolk
1/2 cup rum

Preheat oven to 350F (175C). Butter a 9-inch square baking dish. Combine all ingredients in a large bowl—the mixture should be moist but not soupy. Pour into buttered dish and set on middle rack of oven.

Bake in preheated oven 1-1/4 hours, or until top is golden brown. While pudding is baking, prepare sauce. Cut bread pudding into squares and serve on a dessert dish. Top each square with warm sauce. *Makes about 20 servings.*

Rum Sauce

Cream butter and sugar in a saucepan over medium heat until all butter is absorbed. Remove from heat and blend in egg yolk, then pour in rum while stirring constantly. The sauce will thicken as it cools from hot to warm.

ISLAND PARFAITS

The grated coconut proves the perfect finish for these cooling Caribbean parfaits.

1/2 large fresh pineapple, peeled, cored, cubed
2 papayas, peeled, seeded, cubed
1 mango, peeled, pitted, chopped
1 banana
1/2 cup freshly squeezed orange juice
1/2 cup grated coconut

In a large bowl, combine pineapple, papaya and mango. In a food processor or blender, combine banana and orange juice; process until smooth. Fill tall dessert glasses halfway with fruit, then top off with banana mixture, stirring each just enough to mix. Cover with plastic wrap and chill several hours to blend flavors. When ready to serve, sprinkle top of each dessert with grated coconut. *Makes 6 servings.*

PINEAPPLE RICE PUDDING

The Spanish, of course, have long loved their dessert called *arroz con leche.* Yet here, thanks to its sojourn in the Caribbean, the dish takes a delightful tropical turn.

2 cups cooked rice
3 cups milk
1/3 cup plus 2 tablespoons sugar
2 tablespoons butter
1/2 teaspoon salt
3 eggs, separated
1 (20-oz.) can crushed pineapple, with juice reserved
1-1/2 teaspoons vanilla extract
1/2 cup flaked coconut
1 tablespoon cornstarch
1/4 cup packed brown sugar

Combine rice, 2-1/2 cups milk, 1/3 cup sugar, 1 tablespoon butter and salt in a 2-quart saucepan. Cook over medium heat, stirring occasionally, until thick and creamy, about 20 minutes. Beat egg yolks with remaining milk, add to rice mixture and cook 1 minute more. Remove from heat, then add pineapple and 1 teaspoon vanilla. Cool.

Preheat oven to 325F (165C). Butter a 13 x 9-inch baking dish. In a bowl, beat egg whites and remaining 2 tablespoons sugar until peaks are stiff but not dry. Fold into cooled rice mixture and turn into buttered baking dish. Sprinkle with coconut.

Bake in preheated oven 20 to 25 minutes. Meanwhile, combine reserved pineapple juice with cornstarch in a 1-quart saucepan, stirring to dissolve cornstarch. Add remaining 1 tablespoon butter, brown sugar and a pinch of salt. Cook, stirring frequently, until clear and thickened. Add remaining 1/2 teaspoon of vanilla. Spoon sauce over warm pudding. *Makes 6 servings.*

TIE-A-LEAF

This fascinating sweet comes all the way from West Africa. Nearly every island cook calls it something different, *dokono* being the Fanti tribe's word and "blue drawers" being popular as well. I think Tie-a-Leaf is the most Caribbean, though, offering a kind of poetry in motion.

1 pound cornmeal (3 cups)
1/4 cup all-purpose flour
1 cup sugar
1/2 cup grated coconut
1 teaspoon ground cinnamon
1 teaspoon ground allspice
1 teaspoon salt
1 tablespoon molasses
2 tablespoons vanilla extract
2-1/2 cups Coconut Milk (page 26)

Blend thoroughly cornmeal, flour, sugar, grated coconut, cinnamon, allspice and salt. In a separate bowl, mix molasses, vanilla and Coconut Milk. Add this liquid to dry ingredients, stirring briskly.

Place 1/2 cup of mixture into banana leaves that have been lightly boiled until pliable or into aluminum foil, fold sides up around mixture and tie together with banana bark or twine. Place parcels in enough boiling water to cover and cook 40 minutes. *Makes 8 servings.*

TRIFLE

The English taught the Caribbean how to make and love trifle, but the islanders themselves discovered how to weave the best local ingredients into the traditional mix.

5 egg yolks
1/4 cup sugar
1 pinch of salt
1 cup milk
1/2 pint (1 cup) whipping cream
2 tablespoons dark rum
1 Sponge Cake (page 172)
1/2 cup dark rum
6 pineapple slices
1 cup strawberries, sliced
1/2 pint (1 cup) whipping cream
2 tablespoons sugar
1 tablespoon dark rum
1 mango, sliced

To prepare custard, combine egg yolks, sugar and salt in top of a double boiler; beat with a wire whisk until pale and creamy. Combine milk and cream in a medium saucepan and bring to a boil, then slowly pour this into egg mixture, stirring constantly. Put top of double boiler over hot but not boiling water and cook, stirring constantly, until the mixture thickens lightly and just coats a metal spoon. Remove from heat and stir in 2 tablespoons rum. Cool.

To assemble trifle, slice cake in half and set bottom half in a 9-inch serving bowl or soufflé dish. Sprinkle this layer with 1/4 cup rum, then cover with sliced pineapple. Set top half of cake on pineapple, sprinkle with 1/4 cup rum and cover with custard. Cover with plastic wrap. Refrigerate 3 to 4 hours.

To serve, whip cream in a chilled medium bowl until soft peaks form, then beat in sugar and final 1 tablespoon rum. Cover surface of custard with cream, smoothing it with a rubber spatula. Decorate with mango slices. *Makes 8 to 10 servings.*

Seville Orange Tart

As the name alludes, the Spanish brought oranges along with so many other fruits to the Caribbean. They turned the islands into a garden to feed their far-flung empire.

1/4 cup butter
1 tablespoon grated orange peel
1/4 cup orange juice
1/4 cup light rum
1 pinch of salt
3/4 cup sugar
2 egg yolks
3 eggs
1/2 cup whipping cream
1 baked Pie Crust (page 182)

Glazed Orange Slices

1/4 cup water
1 cup sugar
1 orange, thinly sliced

Melt butter in top of a double boiler over simmering water, then add orange peel, juice, rum, salt and sugar. Beat together yolks and whole eggs, then add them to mixture. Cook over hot water, stirring constantly, until mixture is thick and shiny. Spoon into a bowl; cool.

In a chilled small bowl, whip cream until it is very thick, then fold into orange mixture. Fill pie crust. Make Glazed Orange Slices. Garnish tart with Glazed Orange Slices. *Makes 1 (9-inch) tart.*

Glazed Orange Slices

Bring water and sugar to a boil in a small saucepan. Reduce heat and simmer 2 to 3 minutes. Dip orange slices in syrup for 1 minute; cool on plastic wrap.

GIZADAS

Islanders are notorious snackers. Here is one of their simplest and best snacks.

1 large coconut, grated
2/3 cup packed brown sugar
1/2 teaspoon freshly grated nutmeg
1 recipe Pie Crust (page 182)

Preheat oven to 375F (190C). Grease a baking sheet. In a large bowl, mix coconut, brown sugar and nutmeg. Pinch off small balls of pie crust dough and roll out into 3-inch circles. Pinch edges to form a ridge around outer edge of each, then fill with coconut mixture. Place on greased baking sheet. Bake in preheated oven until pastry is golden, about 20 minutes. *Makes 6 to 8 servings.*

SWEET POTATO PIE

This pie was such a favorite of African slaves that it survives today not only in Caribbean cuisine but as a preferred dessert in "soulfood" restaurants in major American cities.

1 tablespoon butter, softened
2 cups mashed, cooked sweet potatoes
2 eggs, beaten
1 cup evaporated milk
3/4 cup packed light brown sugar
1/2 cup light corn syrup
1 teaspoon vanilla extract
1/2 teaspoon ground ginger
1/2 teaspoon ground cinnamon
1/2 teaspoon freshly grated nutmeg
1 unbaked Pie Crust (page 182)
Whipped cream

Preheat oven to 375F (190C). Beat butter, sweet potatoes and eggs in a medium bowl until combined. Mix in evaporated milk, brown sugar, corn syrup, vanilla, ginger, cinnamon and nutmeg. Pour mixture into pie shell. Bake in preheated oven 35 to 45 minutes. Decorate with whipped cream. *Makes 1 pie.*

SWEET POTATO PONE

Here is a variation on the pie above. Like any terrific pudding or pone, it is baked without a pie crust. And the coconut and raisins give it an extra dash of flavor.

1 pound raw sweet potatoes, grated
1 cup milk
1 cup cream of coconut
1-1/4 cups packed light brown sugar
1 teaspoon vanilla extract
1 teaspoon ground ginger
1 teaspoon ground cinnamon
1/2 teaspoon freshly grated nutmeg
1/4 cup raisins
1/4 cup flaked coconut
2 cups hot water
2 tablespoons butter, melted

Preheat oven to 375F (190C). Butter a 2-quart casserole dish. Combine sweet potato, milk, cream of coconut, sugar, vanilla and spices in a medium bowl. Mix well. Add raisins, coconut, hot water and butter, mixing thoroughly. Taste for sweetness and add additional brown sugar if desired. Pour into dish. Bake 50 to 60 minutes or until set. *Makes 6 servings*.

COLD RUM SOUFFLÉ

This cold soufflé is true Caribbean, from its allspice and lime juice to its dark rum.

1 (1/4-oz.) envelope unflavored gelatin
1 cup milk
3/4 cup sugar
4 eggs, separated
1 teaspoon ground allspice
2 tablespoons lime juice
1 tablespoon dark rum
1/2 pint (1 cup) whipping cream

Wrap a 3-inch-wide by 22-inch-long strip of double thickness foil around a 4-cup soufflé dish so it extends 1-1/2 inches above the rim. Fasten with tape and set dish aside.

In a small saucepan, combine gelatin with milk. Let stand 1 minute to soften, then stir in 1/2 cup of sugar. Cook over medium heat, stirring constantly, until gelatin and sugar dissolve. Quickly whisk some of hot milk mixture into a bowl containing egg yolks, then stir egg yolk mixture into saucepan. Add allspice and cook, stirring constantly, until custard thickens slightly, about 2 minutes. Remove from heat, then stir in lime juice and rum. Transfer to a large bowl and chill until mixture mounds on a spoon.

In a separate bowl, beat egg whites until foamy. Gradually add remaining 1/4 cup sugar, beating until stiff but not dry. In a chilled medium bowl, beat cream until stiff. Fold whipped cream and beaten egg whites into gelatin mixture. Spoon into prepared soufflé dish and refrigerate until firm, about 3 hours. To serve, remove foil collar.   *Makes 6 to 8 servings.*

NOTE: This recipe uses raw egg whites, which should not be eaten by anyone with a serious illness, the elderly or the very young.

ROYAL PINES

On English-speaking islands, pineapples are usually called just "pines." This frozen dessert is usually called just wonderful.

6 small pineapples
1 pint vanilla ice cream, softened
1/2 pint (1 cup) whipping cream, whipped
3 tablespoons light rum
1/2 teaspoon ground mace
1/4 teaspoon ground ginger
1/2 cup diced bananas
1/2 cup diced orange sections
1/2 cup sliced strawberries

Cut off pineapple tops, wrap them in foil and chill for later use. Scoop out pineapple pulp, leaving shells about 1/2 inch thick. Chill these as well.

In a large bowl, combine pineapple pulp with all remaining ingredients. Fill pineapple shells with this mixture and return to freezer until firm. Replace pineapple tops when ready to serve. *Makes 6 servings.*

Isle of Spice Squares

For the longest time, Grenada was known as the Isle of Spice in honor of all the flavorings cultivated there. These squares not only pay tribute to that tradition—they are devoured regularly in Grenada today.

2-1/2 cups all-purpose flour
1-1/2 teaspoons baking soda
1-1/2 teaspoons ground allspice
1 teaspoon ground ginger
1/4 teaspoon salt
1 cup molasses
1 cup milk
1/2 cup butter, softened
1/2 cup packed dark brown sugar
1 egg

Preheat oven to 325F (165C). Grease a 9-inch square pan, then line it with waxed paper and grease again. Set pan aside. Sift flour, baking soda, allspice, ginger and salt together. In a small bowl, combine molasses and milk. Cream butter in a large bowl. Add brown sugar and beat until fluffy, then beat in egg. Alternately beat in 1/3 of flour mixture with 1/2 of molasses mixture. Repeat, ending with flour. Pour into prepared pan.

Bake 65 to 70 minutes, until a cake tester inserted in center comes out clean. Cool in pan 10 minutes. Loosen with a spatula, then turn onto a wire rack to cool. *Cut into 36 (1-1/2-inch) squares.*

Mango Sherbet

Sherbets, sometimes called *sorbets* in the French fashion, are gaining popularity in the Caribbean and Stateside as refreshments to serve between courses.

1 cup sugar
1 (1/4-oz.) envelope unflavored gelatin
1-1/2 cups boiling water
1-1/2 cups mango puree (2 to 3 mangoes)
1 cup milk
2 tablespoons freshly squeezed lime juice
2 egg whites

In a large bowl, combine 3/4 cup of sugar with gelatin. Add boiling water, stirring until sugar and gelatin dissolve completely. Cool to room temperature. Stir in mango puree, milk and lime juice. Place bowl in freezer for 1-1/2 hours, or until mixture is frozen about 1/2 inch around sides of bowl. Beat with a whisk until smooth.

In a separate bowl, beat egg whites with remaining 1/4 cup sugar until stiff peaks form, then fold into mango mixture. Return sherbet to freezer for several more hours, or until firm.   *Makes 1-1/2 quarts.*

NOTE: This recipe uses raw egg whites, which should not be eaten by anyone with a serious illness, the elderly or the very young.

COCONUT COOKIES

It didn't take any great genius to think of putting coconut in cookies. It just took a cook with plenty of coconut.

1 cup all-purpose flour
1-1/2 teaspoons baking powder
1/2 cup sugar
2 tablespoons shortening
1/2 cup grated coconut
1 teaspoon vanilla extract
1 egg white, lightly beaten

Preheat oven to 400F (205C). Sift flour, baking powder and sugar into a medium bowl. Cut in shortening until mixture resembles peas, then stir in coconut and vanilla. Stir egg white into mixture.

Knead dough on a lightly floured board until it is smooth. Roll out 1/4 inch thick on a lightly floured board. Cut into 1-1/2-inch shapes (a mixture of rounds, rectangles and triangles increases eye appeal) and set on a greased baking sheet. Bake 12 to 15 minutes, until golden brown. *Makes about 24 cookies.*

NUTMEG ICE CREAM

This wonderful ice cream from Grenada is easier than ever with the wide variety of home ice-cream makers on the market.

2 cups milk
1 cup half and half
4 large eggs
3/4 cup sugar
3/4 cup sweetened condensed milk
2 medium whole nutmegs, freshly grated
1-1/2 cups whipping cream

In a large saucepan over low heat, combine milk and half and half. Bring mixture just to point at which steam rises to surface. Do not boil. Meanwhile, in a medium bowl, thoroughly blend eggs and sugar. Whisk a small amount of hot milk into egg-sugar mixture, then pour mixture into saucepan with remaining milk and cook, stirring constantly, over low heat until consistency of custard. Do not boil.

Remove mixture from heat, stir in condensed milk and nutmeg and cool to room temperature. Stir cream into cooled nutmeg mixture and refrigerate 2 hours. Freeze in a half-gallon ice-cream maker according to manufacturer's instructions. *Makes 8 servings.*

BLUE MOUNTAIN MOUSSE

This mousse tastes dramatically of coffee, a tribute not only to the Blue Mountains but to the importance of the bean in Caribbean history and economics.

4 eggs, separated
1/2 cup sugar
1/2 cup coffee
2 tablespoons Tia Maria liqueur
2 teaspoons unflavored gelatin powder
Shaved chocolate
Whipped cream

Beat egg yolks and sugar in a medium bowl until pale and fluffy. Mix coffee and Tia Maria in a small saucepan. Sprinkle with gelatin. Set aside 5 minutes to soften. Cook over medium heat, stirring constantly, just until gelatin dissolves. Add gelatin mixture to egg yolks and cool. Beat egg whites until they are stiff but not dry and fold them into mousse. Spoon into individual dessert glasses and garnish with chocolate and whipped cream. *Makes 6 servings*.

NOTE: This recipe uses raw egg whites, which should not be eaten by anyone with a serious illness, the elderly or the very young.

COFFEE CLOUDS

This light and fluffy dessert is perfect for entertaining since it can be made ahead.

1/2 cup water
1 (1/4-oz.) package unflavored gelatin
2-1/2 teaspoons instant espresso coffee powder
4 egg yolks
2 eggs
2/3 cup sugar
1 tablespoon Kahlua or other coffee liqueur
1 pint (2 cups) whipping cream
Shaved chocolate

Pour water into a small saucepan and sprinkle with gelatin. Set aside 5 minutes to soften. Cook over medium heat, stirring constantly, just until gelatin dissolves. Stir in coffee powder, set aside and let cool slightly. In top half of a double boiler set over simmering water, combine egg yolks, eggs and sugar. With a whisk or hand-held electric mixer, beat mixture until very light and fluffy and barely warm to touch, about 5 minutes. Remove top of double boiler and continue beating until mixture has cooled, about 5 minutes more. Transfer to a large bowl. With a rubber spatula, fold in cooled coffee mixture and coffee liqueur. In a chilled bowl, whip cream until soft peaks form. Gently fold cream into coffee mixture. Spoon into 8 large wine goblets or parfait glasses, cover and refrigerate at least 4 hours, preferably overnight. Garnish with shaved chocolate when ready to serve. *Makes 8 servings.*

Black Pudding

Jamaica always springs into my mind around Christmastime. After all, where else can you indulge in English Christmas pudding with none of the moist miseries of English winter? Despite the traditional blueprint, however, you will notice more Caribbean spice in this make-ahead version, along with the substitution of omnipresent rum for rare brandy.

1/2 cup all-purpose flour
1 teaspoon ground allspice
1 teaspoon ground cinnamon
1 teaspoon freshly grated nutmeg
1/2 cup mixed candied peel
1/2 cup chopped blanched almonds
1 tablespoon molasses
1/2 cup unseasoned dry bread crumbs
1/2 cup butter, melted
1/2 cup packed brown sugar
1/2 cup grated apple
1 small carrot, grated
1 cup dark raisins
1/2 cup golden raisins
1/2 cup currants
Grated peel and juice of 1 lemon
2 eggs
2 cups dark rum
Additional rum for flaming

Hard Sauce

1/2 cup butter
3/4 cup powdered sugar
1/4 cup dark rum

In a large bowl, stir all the pudding ingredients together. For a real traditional memory, get each family member to provide one stir, each making a wish as he or she does so. Refrigerate the mixture 24 hours so it can "mature."

Press the pudding mixture into a 2-quart heatproof bowl and cover with waxed paper. Secure the paper with a string. Steam the pudding in its bowl on a rack over boiling water 6 to 8 hours. Remove the damp cover and, when cooled, set on dry paper. Wrap and store in a cool place up to 2 months. On Christmas Day, steam the pudding 2 or 3 hours to make sure it is heated through.

Prepare the sauce and chill. When ready to serve, arrange the pudding on a platter. Heat a ladle of rum, then ignite with care using a long-stemmed match. Pour the flaming liquid over the top of the pudding. Let the flame burn out, then top each serving of pudding with a dollop of hard sauce. *Makes 16 servings.*

HARD SAUCE

Beat the butter in a medium bowl until it is light and fluffy. Gradually beat in the sugar and rum. Refrigerate until hard.

MANGOES & CREAM

You know all about peaches and cream. So take a trip to the islands instead.

2 large mangoes
1/2 pint (1 cup) whipping cream
1 cup plain yogurt
Brown sugar

Peel mangoes and cut pulp into slices. Place slices in 6 individual serving dishes. In a bowl, beat cream until it is thick, then add yogurt. Beat again until mixture is free of lumps. Pour over fruit and then sprinkle liberally with brown sugar. Refrigerate 4 to 5 hours and serve cold. *Makes 6 servings.*

ISLAND DRINKS

Somewhere along the way, the botanical name for sugar *(saccharum officinarum)* was shortened to just plain "rum"—perhaps in deference to those who enjoy it in bulk. At any rate, rum, the fermented, distilled and aged by-product of molasses, which itself is a by-product of sugar, has been part of the Caribbean since the English introduced it in the 1600s. Just about every island has its own proud style of rum-making, and just about every islander will tell you his native rum is best in all the world.

The most reasonable advice, of course, is to drink the rum you like best, whether it hails from Puerto Rico, Jamaica, Barbados or any other Caribbean island. Here is a collection of the most exciting drinks I've tasted over the years. Try them to catch the spirit (though not at a single sitting), then feel free to create your own.

CAFE TRADE WIND

Orange peel and aromatic bitters give a distinctly exotic flavor to this popular island coffee.

4 cups hot coffee
1/4 cup thinly sliced orange peel
1 orange, peeled, sliced
1 tablespoon sugar
1 teaspoon aromatic bitters
1/2 cup whipping cream, whipped

Measure coffee into a flameproof glass pot. Add orange peel and orange slices, steeping over low heat 15 minutes. Add sugar and bitters, then strain and pour into warmed heatproof glasses. Top with whipped cream. *Makes 6 servings.*

COFFEE GROG

Though anything but Iced Coffee, this one might be called Spiced Coffee, for all its spices from the islands. The word "grog," of course, links it to the Caribbean pirate tradition.

1/3 cup packed brown sugar
1 tablespoon butter
1/8 teaspoon ground cinnamon
1/8 teaspoon freshly grated nutmeg
1/8 teaspoon ground cloves
1/8 teaspoon ground allspice
4-1/2 cups hot coffee
3/4 cup dark rum
3/4 cup half and half
6 orange peel twists

In a medium bowl, cream together sugar and butter, then thoroughly blend in spices. Add coffee, rum and half and half, blending well. Ladle mixture into 6 warmed coffee mugs and garnish each serving with an orange peel twist. *Makes 6 servings.*

FLAMING RUM COFFEE

Every culture needs at least one coffee beverage that burns with high drama. What could be more appropriate to ignite here than rum!

6 teaspoons sugar
3-1/2 cups hot coffee
6 tablespoons rum

Place 1 teaspoon of sugar in each of 6 demitasse cups, then fill each 3/4 full with coffee. Float 1 tablespoon of rum on top of each cup and ignite with a long-stemmed match. When flames have burned out, stir coffee, rum and sugar together. *Makes 6 servings.*

JAMAICAN COFFEE

Nothing could be more Jamaican than Tia Maria, perhaps the island's single best known export.

6 cups hot coffee
3/4 cup Tia Maria liqueur
Sugar to taste

Fill 6 warmed cups 3/4 full of hot coffee, then pour in Tia Maria to top. Sweeten lightly with sugar and serve. *Makes 6 servings.*

PLANTER'S PUNCH

Here is a delightful cooler of the sort that helped many a Caribbean land-owner make it through the summer.

2 tablespoons sugar
1/2 tablespoon lime juice
2 tablespoons water
1/4 cup light rum
1 pineapple slice
Crushed ice
1 maraschino cherry

Mix together sugar, lime juice, water and rum in a measuring cup until sugar is dissolved. Chop pineapple and add it to liquid. Fill a tall glass with crushed ice. Pour rum mixture over ice; garnish with cherry. *Makes 1 drink.*

PAPAYA & STRAWBERRY DAIQUIRI

Daiquiries, of course, crossed to the mainland long ago. Here's one, how-ever, that still carries an element of surprise.

1/4 cup papaya puree
1 tablespoon lime juice
2 tablespoons sugar
1 tablespoon strawberry syrup
2 tablespoons light rum
Crushed ice

Combine all ingredients in a blender. Process until blended. Serve in a 10-ounce glass. *Makes 1 drink.*

ALMOND TREE DELIGHT

This orange-pink wonder is a specialty of the Almond Tree Restaurant in Ocho Rios, Jamaica.

2 tablespoons Appleton Special Rum
1 tablespoon Appleton White Rum
2 tablespoons Garniers Cherry Liqueur
2 dashes strawberry syrup
1/2 cup orange juice
1 splash lime juice
Crushed ice
Hibiscus blossom
Orange slice
Maraschino cherry

Combine rum, liqueur, syrup, juices and ice in a blender; blend until smooth. Pour into a tall glass. Garnish with hibiscus blossom, orange slice and cherry. *Makes 1 drink.*

RUM COLLINS

In this variation on the Tom Collins, the rum carries out a Caribbean theme.

2 tablespoons lime juice
2 tablespoons sugar
1/4 cup rum
Crushed ice
Soda water
Lime slices

Stir together lime juice, sugar and rum in a measuring cup until sugar is dissolved. Fill a tall glass with ice. Pour mixture over ice and add a splash of soda water. Garnish with lime slices. *Makes 1 drink.*

POINCIANA AWAKEN

As in most places that have tempting drinks for night, there are throughout the islands numerous "remedies" for the morning after.

1 tablespoon Tia Maria liqueur
2 tablespoons scotch
1 tablespoon Doctor Sangster's Coconut Rum
3 tablespoons whipping cream
1 dash Simple Syrup (page 216)
Freshly grated nutmeg
Hibiscus blossom
Maraschino cherry
Small sugar cane piece

Combine liqueur, scotch, rum, cream and syrup in a blender; blend until smooth. Pour into a glass and top with nutmeg. Garnish with hibiscus blossom, cherry and sugar cane. *Makes 1 drink.*

REGGAE SUNSPLASH

Jamaicans love their funky annual music festival called Reggae Sunsplash. They also love this, its alcoholic namesake.

2 tablespoons lime juice
2 tablespoons strawberry syrup
1/4 cup pineapple juice
2 tablespoons Silver Label Rum
1 tablespoon yellow Chartreuse
Crushed ice

Stir all ingredients except ice together until uniform in color. Fill a tall glass with ice. Pour drink over ice. *Makes 1 drink.*

Sun Island Punch

Here's a bright yellow chiller that showcases the flavors of four different fruits.

1 tablespoon Coruba White Rum
1/2 tablespoon Coruba Gold Rum
1 tablespoon Garnier's Apricot Liqueur
1/4 cup orange juice
1 tablespoon pineapple juice
1 splash lime juice
2 splashes Simple Syrup (page 216)
Crushed ice
Maraschino cherry
Orange slice
Pineapple slice

Combine rums, liqueur, juices, syrup and ice in a blender; blend until smooth. Serve in a tall glass. Spear cherry, orange slice and pineapple slice with a wooden pick; use to garnish drink. *Makes 1 drink.*

Shady Island

Despite its name, this drink ends up an intense red, the result of orange juice enlivened by strawberry syrup.

2 tablespoons Coruba Dark Rum
1 tablespoon Bols Blackberry Brandy
1 tablespoon Doctor Sangster's Orange Coffee Liqueur
2 dashes strawberry syrup
1/2 cup orange juice
1 dash lime juice
Crushed ice

Combine all ingredients in a blender; blend until smooth. Serve in a tall glass. *Makes 1 drink.*

COCONUT HEART

This frothy drink not only features coconut rum but is served in a coconut shell.

2 tablespoons Doctor Sangster's Coconut Rum
1 tablespoon Doctor Sangster's Wild Orange Liqueur
2 dashes Simple Syrup (page 216)
1/2 cup pineapple juice
Crushed ice
Pineapple chunks
Banana slices
Maraschino cherry

    Swizzle rum, liqueur, syrup, juice and ice together and serve, preferably in a coconut shell. Garnish with a swizzle stick skewering pineapple chunks, banana slices and a cherry. *Makes 1 drink*.

RUM PUNCH

Every islander has a favorite rum punch. Now you will have one, too.

Crushed ice
2 tablespoons lime juice
1/4 cup Simple Syrup (page 216)
1/2 cup light rum
1/2 cup fruit juice of your choice
Pineapple chunks
Lemon or lime slice

    Fill a tall glass with ice. Thoroughly mix remaining ingredients except pineapple and lemon slice and pour over crushed ice. Garnish with pineapple, lemon or lime. *Makes 1 serving*.

MISTY MOOD

To islanders, this seems the perfect drink to sip while gazing out at a calm sea.

2 tablespoons Appleton Gold Rum
1 tablespoon Bols Creme de Banana
1 tablespoon Tia Maria liqueur
1/4 cup whipping cream
1/4 cup pineapple juice
2 dashes Simple Syrup (page 216)
Crushed ice
Hibiscus blossom
Maraschino cherry
Banana slices

Combine rum, creme de banana, liqueur, cream, juice, syrup and ice in a blender; blend together until smooth. Serve in a tall glass. Garnish with hibiscus blossom, cherry and banana slices. *Makes 1 drink.*

SANGAREE

While the Caribbean people love the same frothy blender drinks they serve to tourists, they also have simpler tastes—like this old-fashioned refresher from the British islands.

Crushed ice
1/4 cup sherry
1/2 cup water
Sugar
Grated nutmeg
1 lime slice

Fill a tall glass with ice. Mix together sherry and water and pour over ice. Sweeten to taste with sugar and sprinkle with nutmeg. Garnish with lime slice. *Makes 1 drink.*

Song of Happiness

Yellow seems to be the "happy color" in the Caribbean, making this drink happy indeed.

1 tablespoon Doctor Sangster's Orange Coffee Liqueur
1 tablespoon Doctor Sangster's Ortanique Liqueur
2 tablespoons Appleton Gold Rum
1 dash lime juice
1/4 cup pineapple juice
Crushed ice
Pineapple chunks
Banana slice
Maraschino cherry

Stir liqueurs, rum, juices and ice together. Serve in a tall glass. Garnish with a swizzle stick skewering pineapple chunks, banana slices and cherry. *Makes 1 serving.*

Fruit Punch

Strawberry syrup is available at stores that sell Caribbean foods.

6 cups orange juice
2 cups pineapple juice
1 cup guava nectar
1 cup brewed tea
Strawberry syrup (optional)

Mix together all ingredients. Let stand at least 30 minutes before serving over ice. *Makes 10 servings.*

ANNIE'S ITCH

The name of this concoction recalls the White Witch of Rose Hall, who allegedly still haunts her Jamaican great house near Montego Bay.

2 tablespoons lime juice
2 tablespoons Simple Syrup (below)
1/2 cup orange juice
2 tablespoons Ovenproof Rum
1 tablespoon brown Creme de Cacao
Crushed ice

Combine all ingredients in a blender; blend until smooth. Serve in a snifter. *Makes 1 serving.*

SIMPLE SYRUP

Combine equal portions of sugar and water in a saucepan. Bring to a boil, stirring until sugar dissolves. Cool. Refrigerate until needed.

CARROT DRINK

A rich-tasting milk drink that's good for you.

2 cups diced carrots
2 cups water
1 cup evaporated milk
7 tablespoons sugar
1/4 teaspoon freshly grated nutmeg
1 teaspoon vanilla extract
4 ice cubes

Combine the carrots and water in a blender, cover and blend 30 seconds. Strain and rinse the blender jar. Return the carrot juice and remaining ingredients to blender. Blend again and serve chilled. *Makes 6 servings.*

INGREDIENTS

Though I've taken the poetic (or culinary) license to translate these island drink recipes from jiggers and ounces to cups and tablespoons, I've chosen to retain the specific liquor brand names. Liquor has long been one of our most widely distributed products, making most of these items fairly easy to find. In addition, these are the precise ingredients favored by the Caribbean barman who came up with each drink. Each creator, of course, would swear on a stack of cocktail napkins you must use his chosen brand. The fact is, though, if you know your way around a liquor cabinet, you can make some intelligent substitutions.

RUMONA FLIP

Here's a nifty creation named after a popular island liqueur.

2 tablespoons lime juice
2 tablespoons strawberry syrup
1/2 cup pineapple juice
2 tablespoons light rum
1 tablespoon Rumona Liqueur
Strawberry

In a shaker or blender, mix together all ingredients except strawberry. Serve in a tall glass. Garnish with a strawberry. *Makes 1 serving.*

HIBISCUS MIST

Blackberry brandy helps give color to this unusual combination, while the amaretto adds substance.

1 tablespoon Bols Blackberry Brandy
1 dash amaretto liqueur
2 tablespoons Coruba Gold Rum
1 dash lime juice
1/2 cup pineapple juice
2 dashes Simple Syrup (page 216)
Crushed ice
Hibiscus blossom
Small sugar cane stick

Combine all ingredients except hibiscus blossom and sugar cane; blend until smooth. Garnish with hibiscus blossom and sugar cane stick. *Makes 1 drink.*

BEET DRINK

Condensed milk became popular in the islands before it was possible to store fresh milk. Refrigerate leftover condensed milk up to three days.

1 cup diced beets
2 cups water
1/4 teaspoon freshly grated nutmeg
2 tablespoons sweetened condensed milk
3 cubes ice

Combine the beets and water in a blender, then cover and blend until fine. Strain, rinse the blender jar. Return the beet juice and remaining ingredients to blender. Blend 10 more seconds and serve chilled. *Makes 4 to 6 servings.*

OTAHEITE APPLE DRINK

Otaheite apple is a tropical fruit.

1/2 ounce gingerroot
1 pound sugar
1 quart water
12 ripe otaheite apples
Juice of 2 limes

    Grate the gingerroot. Add the gingerroot and sugar to the water. Chop the apples and sprinkle with the lime juice. In a saucepan, combine the apples with the ginger water, bring to a boil and simmer 20 minutes. Cool and strain. Serve with crushed ice. *Makes 8 servings*.

SOURSOP JUICE

Soursoup is a green heart-shaped fruit grown for use in drinks and desserts.

1 ripe soursop
3 cups water
Sweetened condensed milk to taste
Freshly grated nutmeg to taste
1/2 teaspoon lime juice

    Peel the soursop and remove seeds. Place the water and 1 cup of soursop pulp in a blender. Blend until combined. Strain into a pitcher. Sweeten to taste with condensed milk and stir in nutmeg. Add the lime juice and serve with crushed ice. *Makes 4 servings*.

Caribbean Lemonade

Tart and refreshing when the weather is hot and humid.

3 tablespoons sugar
1 pint water
Juice of 2 lemons

Combine the sugar and water, then add the lemon juice. Stir and serve over crushed ice. *Makes 1 or 2 servings.*

Pineapple-Ginger Drink

This uses the part of the pineapple that is usually thrown away.

Rinsed peel and leftover pulp of 1 fresh pineapple
1 (1-inch) piece gingerroot, grated
3 cups boiling water
Sugar to taste

Place the pineapple pieces in a large container with the gingerroot. Add the boiling water and allow to sit overnight. Strain, sweeten to taste and refrigerate. Serve over crushed ice. *Makes 4 servings.*

TAMARIND DRINK

Pods of the tamarind tree contain tart-sweet pulp and seeds.

4 cups shelled tamarind
8 cups water
Sugar to taste

    Combine the tamarinds and the water and allow to sit overnight. Strain, sweeten to taste and refrigerate. Add additional water if too thick. Serve over crushed ice.   *Makes 8 servings.*

Sources

The ingredients used in Caribbean food are becoming easier and easier to find in the supermarket you normally patronize. Yet there are a few elements from some dishes that, on any given day, resist even your best efforts. Here is a list of good starting points in the United States. You can visit them in person if they are in your area, or you can call or write them for shopping advice if they are not.

CALIFORNIA
Casa Lucas Market
2934 24th Street
San Francisco, CA 94110

FLORIDA
Delicatessen, Burdines Dadeland
Dadeland Shopping Center
Miami, FL 33156

Epicure Market
1656 Alton Road
Miami Beach, FL 33139

Smith Knaupp Seafood Company
450 W. McNab Road
Fort Lauderdale, FL 33309

GEORGIA
Helen's Tropical Exotics
c/o Gourmet Concepts
3519 Church Street
Clarkston, GA 30021
404-296-6100

ILLINOIS
La Preferida Inc.
3400 W. 35th Street
Chicago, IL 60632

Marshall Field and Company
111 N. State Street
Chicago, IL 60602

LOUISIANA
Central Grocery
923 Decatur Street
New Orleans, LA 70116
504-523-1620

MICHIGAN
Fox Hill Herb Farm
444 W. Michigan Avenue
Parma, MI 49269

NEW YORK
Brooklyn Terminal
Liberty Avenue
Brooklyn, NY 11207
718-444-5700

Casa Monteo Spanish Imports
210 W. 14th Street
New York, NY 10011

Kalustyan Orient Export Trading Co.
123 Lexington Avenue
New York, NY 10016

WASHINGTON, DC
Continental Trading
7826 Easter Avenue N.W.
Suite 500
Washington, DC 20009
202-829-5620

Metric Conversion Charts

Comparison to Metric Measure

When You Know	Symbol	Multiply By	To Find	Symbol
teaspoons	tsp.	5.0	milliliters	ml
tablespoons	tbsp.	15.0	milliliters	ml
fluid ounces	fl. oz.	30.0	milliliters	ml
cups	c	0.24	liters	l
pints	pt.	0.47	liters	l
quarts	qt.	0.95	liters	l
ounces	oz.	28.0	grams	g
pounds	lb.	0.45	kilograms	kg
Fahrenheit	F	5/9 (after subtracting 32)	Celsius	C

Fahrenheit to Celsius

F	C
200–205	95
220–225	105
245–250	120
275	135
300–305	150
325–330	165
345–350	175
370–375	190
400–405	205
425–430	220
445–450	230
470–475	245
500	260

Liquid Measure to Milliliters

1/4 teaspoon	=	1.25 milliliters
1/2 teaspoon	=	2.5 milliliters
3/4 teaspoon	=	3.75 milliliters
1 teaspoon	=	5.0 milliliters
1-1/4 teaspoons	=	6.25 milliliters
1-1/2 teaspoons	=	7.5 milliliters
1-3/4 teaspoons	=	8.75 milliliters
2 teaspoons	=	10.0 milliliters
1 tablespoon	=	15.0 milliliters
2 tablespoons	=	30.0 milliliters

Liquid Measure to Liters

1/4 cup	=	0.06 liters
1/2 cup	=	0.12 liters
3/4 cup	=	0.18 liters
1 cup	=	0.24 liters
1-1/4 cups	=	0.3 liters
1-1/2 cups	=	0.36 liters
2 cups	=	0.48 liters
2-1/2 cups	=	0.6 liters
3 cups	=	0.72 liters
3-1/2 cups	=	0.84 liters
4 cups	=	0.96 liters
4-1/2 cups	=	1.08 liters
5 cups	=	1.2 liters
5-1/2 cups	=	1.32 liters

INDEX